"Pick up her book... flip to any page, and be inspired!"

Her story is one I believe can be an encouragement to countless people who struggle with the complexities of day-to-day life in our world...I find particularly refreshing the depth of honesty from which she shares...Hers is a faith that has been tried and tested and continues to carry her through.

Zig Ziglar
Author/Motivational Teacher

Some people see life a lot more clearly than others, and my friend Gail McWilliams is one of those 'seers' I love listening to. Her buoyant enthusiasm, infectious faith, and passion to make Jesus real to everyone around her gives Gail an extraordinary insight into the way things are, and the way things should be. Pick up her book, Seeing Beyond, *flip to any page, and be inspired!*

Joni Eareckson Tada
The Joni & Friends International Disability Center

We would be wise to see in Gail's life the impact of a life fully surrendered...regardless of the obstacles and open to Christ-centered possibilities.

Pete Briscoe
Pastor/Author/Radio Host, Bent Tree Bible Fellowship

The One who promised to "turn our sorrows into joy" and exchange our "ashes for beauty" manifests Himself through Gail's life experiences...The old saying, "When trouble moves in, make it pay rent," certainly has proven true in Gail's life. Seeing Beyond *is an inspiring account that will encourage those facing difficult days to use their sorrows rather that waste them.*

Dr. Harold Helms
Pastor/Author/International Board Member
Foursquare Church

Gail captured my imagination and heart, placed me in her life situations, and made me laugh and cry from the beginning to the end.

Lucille Madeira
Co-Founder, Maximize Life

Do you see what I see in this amazing book? I see a beautiful, brave, believer who has battled physical blindness, but who helps all of us see the brilliance of a blessed and balanced life. Look into her heart through this book and envision how you, too, can see more clearly.

Thelma Wells
President A Woman of God Ministries/Speaker/Author

SEEING

BEYOND

SEEING

BEYOND

Choosing to Look Past
the Horizon

GAIL
MᶜWILLIAMS

SEEING BEYOND

© 2006 Gail McWilliams

Written by Gail McWilliams
Cover designed by Ryan Duckworth

Manufactured in the United States of America

Published by
Generations Global Press
www.GenerationsGlobal.com
"...beyond the horizon, around the globe, and to generations yet to come."

For information, please contact:
www.GailMcWilliams.com

Paperback ISBN: 978-0-9799512-8-2
LCCN: 2013948942
1 2 3 4 5 6 7 8 9 10

4th Printing 2014

DEDICATED TO

My husband, Tony, who has faithfully walked with me through every page of this incredible journey. Your courageous love has never wavered for me as you have had to see beyond my imperfections and struggles. I love you.

My children, Anna, Lindey, Holly, Lydia and Connor, who have made each step of this journey worthwhile. I would choose you again in a heartbeat! You are my joy and love.

TABLE OF CONTENTS
SEEING BEYOND

TABLE OF CONTENTS

PREFACE

Everyone has something in his or her life to "see beyond." Life's challenges and disappointments often blur our vision and cause us to lose focus on our journey. No matter what your visual acuity may be or how many lines you can read on the eye chart, I wonder what you really see.

One thing I have learned over the past years is that eyesight has little to do with vision. The former is based on visual ability, while the latter depends on the heart. Vision that sees from the heart can see even when darkness comes. It is fascinating to me that Jesus made an appeal for mankind to look beyond their physical eyesight. He marveled, saying, "You have eyes and yet you do not see." Aren't you curious to ask, "See what?"

Some see only what they want to see while others refuse to see at all. Many overlook the true riches in life, failing to embrace today. Eyes that merely see are common, but rare are the eyes that are "SEEING BEYOND."

ACKNOWLEDGEMENTS

With any successful project there is a valuable team whose contributions help make it excellent. This is the case with my first book. Just beyond the pages I have written are some special people I want to thank.

Thank you, Tony, for not only being my supportive husband but also my manager and key editor. Your long hours and commitment to this project enabled me to finish well. When I overheard you laugh aloud and then cry as you read the manuscript for the first time, it made me hopeful that the book could reach other hearts.

Thank you, dear children, for letting me stay barricaded in the office for the last two months of finishing this book. Anna, Lindey, Holly, Lydia and Connor, your encouragement of my writing this book and your hopes of its being a best seller cheered me on to the finish line.

Thank you, Linda Eisenmayer, for requiring me to write with passion and not merely tell the story. You gave me the courage to revisit some things that I had hoped to suppress in my heart forever.

To all the editing team who crossed my t's and dotted my i's, thank you for your eagle vision.

I salute you, Chet and Janet Moyers, my mom and dad. Your endless love and support for me and the Savior have stretched over a lifetime. Thank you for being the first sets of eyes that helped me look over the manuscript I typed myself. Mom, you have definitely earned the affectionate title "Comma Queen."

Special thanks to my brother, Jon Moyers, who helped with the editing process, including checking timelines and asking investigative questions — like an excellent lawyer would.

Julie Pangrac, your incredible gift for writing and your love for literature and me helped refine the details of the story. Thank you, my friend, for your willingness to spend the long hours to make the story stronger. You were there to cheer me on to write long before I thought I could.

Anna Jean Price, thank you for your editing contributions and endless encouragement.

Ryan Duckworth, thank you for your artist's eye and expertise in designing the book cover. You skillfully captured what I had imagined and made it into a masterpiece.

To all the friends who encouraged me to write, I am grateful. Some of you are deserving of special mention.

Mr. Ziglar, thank you for your love and encouragement. The manuscript was placed on your desk nearly one year from the day when you first stated emphatically, "Gail, you must write your story for the masses." You not only believed in me but helped me see more.

To Laurie Magers, Mr. Ziglar's fantastic assistant, whom I now claim as my insightful friend, I owe a debt of gratitude for your daily encouragement and practical help.

I love you, Debbie Bernard, because you tirelessly persisted in asking if I had started my book and then screamed with joy when it was finally completed. John Childs, your loving, yet stern response to why I didn't think I wanted to write my story was, undoubtedly, the pivotal point in making my decision to try. June Evans, you delivered to me the final motivation to finish when I had become distracted and felt like quitting. Anne Sonnier, your daily e-mails and prayers of encouragement helped me to see beyond the work and focus on His assignment. Dawn, Harriet, Karen and Mrs. M, I heard your cheers from the stands as I smiled at every turn on the track. Thanks to you and the hundreds of others who also stood cheering.

To my friends at HighRidge Church, thank you for your constant excitement and encouragement as you watched this book be born.

Three pastor friends believed in me as they encouraged me to begin to write not only this book but also many more. Dan Dean, thank you for telling me from the pulpit that best sellers were in me, waiting to be written. Clint Collins, your encouragement made me want to reach for the next summit. Brian Holmes, when you placed a pen in my hand as a group of us prayed, I knew my time had come to be obedient. Thank you my brothers and co-laborers in the kingdom.

A special thanks to all who previewed the manuscript, wrote endorsements, and added helpful comments. To you, Mike Kelly, thank you for your endless enthusiasm and practical help for expanding our vision in the marketplace.

I give grateful tribute to the Texas Commission for the Blind who first provided me with a computer and the awesome software that enabled me to begin to type and write once again. Gail Elie, you were the best advocate to get the equipment I needed, as you believed that I would, indeed, write many books. A special thank you goes to Ashley Thomas and the Dallas Lighthouse for the Blind, who gave me extensive computer training. Thanks to Freedom Scientific for developing a specialized software program, J.A.W.S., that keeps me writing in spite of the dark.

My utmost thanks and praise belongs to the Lord Jesus Christ. Without His help the story could not have been told or written. My heart overflows with thanksgiving for all the lives that have been mentioned above. I can't help but think about Psalm 35:18, "I will give You full credit when everyone gathers for worship; when the people turn out in force I will say my Hallelujahs." (MSG)

FOREWORD

BY ZIG ZIGLAR

I am gratified to have had the pleasure and honor of getting to know Gail and Tony McWilliams. Her story is one I believe can be an encouragement to countless people who are struggling with the complexities of day-to-day life in our world.

Gail writes as if she is having a conversation with the reader. It's easy to feel her heart through her words. I find particularly refreshing the depth of her honesty. Growing up in a committed Christian family, making her own decision for Christ as a young girl, and determined to pattern her life after that of our Savior, she encountered the challenges and roadblocks familiar to all, as well as many that were unique to her.

Rather than glossing her difficulties over with platitudes that perhaps have become common among Christian authors, Gail shares with her readers the not-so-pretty side of fear and disappointment—the anger, bitterness, resentment, pain, and frustration she experienced, and even her doubt, especially and particularly with those claiming Christ as Lord. She pulls no punches in expressing the agony of her struggles, and she just as clearly and willingly divulges how she faced—and continues to face--each and every test and trial. Hers is a faith that has been tried and tested and continues to carry her through.

The McWilliams family is a living testimony to the joy that comes only from a personal relationship with our Lord and Savior, Jesus Christ. I believe Seeing Beyond will give you new perspectives on your own journey, and hope and encouragement for what lies ahead.

Zig Ziglar
Author/Motivational Teacher

INTRODUCTION

I nervously watched the clock on the wall, dreading to hear the routine, nightly announcement so frightening to a nine-year-old girl. "Attention. Visiting hours are over." Our time together had expired for one more night, and I would soon be alone.

My face dropped as I watched my parents gather their things to travel the road home without their little girl. Just a few months earlier my parents were considering a possible mission trip to Africa. Their deep commitment to following Christ had inspired them to look for ways to help others. For them, living for Christ was more than attending a few church services a week; instead, it was a lifestyle of reaching to know Him better. That relationship with a living God supported all of us as our family felt the effects of the disease that had rearranged our plans and our lives forever. Who could have imagined that the symptoms of a common flu would really be a childhood illness that we would continually battle. Life would be the prize, but the price paid would be more than any of us could imagine. In innocence, I could only feel the pain of the moment.

The diagnosis of a soon-to-retire doctor had brought me to this medical center. My carefree childhood would be encumbered by daily injections, endless monitoring, and the greatest enemy of all, the feeling of being different from everyone else.

Trying not to cry, I hugged my parents as I sat on the bed. I caught a glimpse of tears in their eyes as their faces changed along with mine. "Let me walk you to the elevator," I pleaded, as I tried to squeeze out more minutes together. As we walked slowly to the end of the hall, my stomach started to roll and the tears began to fall. Though I longed to be well, I also longed to go home. I whispered, "Do you have to go?" No words were exchanged, only tender, long hugs as my dad reluctantly pressed the elevator button. "We'll be back tomorrow."

I painfully watched as the doors opened. I would soon cast off on a voyage that my parents could not control and from which they could not protect me; they could only watch from the shore. My journey would be fully entrusted to the Captain of my destiny, following charted waters of His choosing. The waters would take me to a pleasant place, in time; but, for now, I appeared to be abandoned.

I took one last gaze at the two people I loved most, as the elevator doors closed. I was alone. I stood in the cold sterile hospital hall unable to hold back the tears, unable to see beyond that closed door.

CHAPTER ONE
SEEING BEYOND DARKNESS

Late one March, I traveled with my fiancé to a pre-scheduled, yearly doctor's appointment. For years, due to juvenile diabetes, I had been placed in an intensive eye research program. Each year I was monitored to determine if the disease had affected my sight in any way. Tragically, diabetes is known to be the greatest cause of blindness and visual impairment. These exams were very thorough, causing the days of testing to be grueling and extremely long. I hated them and feared that the doctors, if they looked too hard, would actually find something wrong. My companion for this visit, however, had helped me focus on the brightness of my future, and I didn't dread the exam quite so much since I was with the man I loved. Looking back, I am not certain if my naiveté existed because the doctors had not informed me or because I was in denial over the potential complications of this disease. I was twenty-one years old, consumed with my future plans and not interested in any interruption this disease could manufacture.

I had met Tony McWilliams one year earlier. My life's dream for love and marriage were becoming reality. I had dreamed of marrying a man who would not only share my heart but also my passion for serving Christ. His quiet strength of character and beautiful blue eyes only enhanced the fulfillment of this dream that I had carried since a young girl. It seems strange now that I had ever doubted I would find such a man. Our future together not only connected two lives but also connected two destinies. I was filled with joy, anticipating the day that I would soon be his wife.

During the drive to the Midwest hospital, we had made lists of last minute details that needed our attention before the day of our wedding. It only seemed appropriate to be planning our wedding while we drove down the highway. For the past three years we had both traveled throughout the United States in our individual ministries. Tony's focus was an evangelistic thrust to college campuses. Mine was to churches where I sang and spoke. Our courtship had been nine months of letter writing and phone calls. Our lives were going to merge two road ministries into one, and we could not wait. We were excited and very much in love.

The entire day at the medical center was consumed with various visual tests, pupil dilation, investigative pictures of my eyes, and lengthy monitoring. We sat among other research patients, and our care seemed impersonal as the medical research staff called each of our numbers.

Our daylight hours had slipped from us. It was as though we'd been taken prisoner, locked in a windowless clinic in the center of the hospital complex and forced to wait for the day's results. At last, my name was called. I quickly and cheerfully informed the nurse that she would have to change my last name on her records by the time I saw her next. I was about to be a bride.

Within minutes, my happiness would be challenged. The presiding doctor gravely warned that a slight change in my eyes had been detected. He explained some of what he saw in the fragile, compromised blood vessels behind my eyes. He resolutely stated, "You will inevitably see blindness in your lifetime." No one knew exactly when. There would be no warning. The storm in my eyes was pending until some future time, which no one could predict.

Together, as we heard the news, we anchored ourselves to a faithful God who could do the impossible. Besides, we were focused only on our new love for one another.

The next hour became a blur as an ominous cloud began to form over us. I felt anxious as I tried to find a place to file away the doctor's report. If only I could shred the memory of his prognosis.

We drove into the dark night with our hearts too numb to form words. I painfully reflected on the doctor's observations as I wondered if the very man now driving me home would still want to marry me in three short weeks. We had heard the warnings from the skilled medical staff that told us of looming clouds of uncertainty. The sun was attempting to set without warning on the horizon of my bright future. I finally found the courage to softly say, "Tony, you don't have to marry me."

We sat voiceless as we drove down the highway, held captive by our own thoughts. Our trip was half over when we exited onto a two-lane road, one hour from home. An eerie darkness broke our silence. "All of the lights are out and the power lines are snapped in two." Everyone appeared to be missing. It was like a plague that blanketed our world. The darkness was blinding.

The scenes were like that of ghost towns nestled in a twilight zone as we passed through one small town after another, each identical. They were in stark contrast to the noisy, bustling city we had left earlier. There wasn't a trace of life anywhere as our tires suddenly skated onto a thick, unexpected ice covering. Clueless as to any impending danger, we inched our way down the faintly traced path. Since our day had been spent in the corridors of a major hospital in the Midwest, we were oblivious to any weather warnings or threatening storms. After all, it was spring and winter's grip had been loosened, marked by the changing pages of the calendar. Mother Nature, however, had surprised her residents with a wintry blast that would be unforgettable.

Creeping along, we marveled at the deep hole of darkness that was coupled with deafening silence. The ice continued to increase with each passing hour, and I wondered at what point we would find relief from the storm's rage. We saw firsthand the devastating damage to our state. The Illinois fields were trapped in thick ice and the power lines lay frayed and lifeless beside the fallen poles.

How had we missed the warning signs? The journey that should have taken only two hours had become a five-hour, tension-filled trip. There were no cell phones at the time, so we could reach no one, nor did anyone know if we were safe. My heart's quest has always been to make a memory, but this was a bit off the charts.

We were only a few weeks from our spring wedding. Now, I watched my fiancé fight to hold the wheel as he steered his future bride to safety. This had been a day of constant heaviness and potential sadness. Now this. Could this darkness and severe storm be a forewarning of a life-storm that lay ahead of us? "Oh, God, we are in desperate need of Your help."

Finally, we were close to home, anticipating the greetings of my anxious parents. I underestimated their trials during the storm, however. Due to the extensive power outage in the region, the sump pump in the basement wasn't working and water had mercilessly flooded our finished basement. They had been bailing water all night.

My wedding dress had been hanging in the basement with the hem carefully spread out on a white sheet. It was pressed and awaiting the celebration of marriage to the man I loved. Now, the bottom of my dress was stained with dirty water bubbling up from the ground. This was more than I could bear when we finally arrived home.

With diligence, we worked as a team and the basement was saved. We moved my soiled dress to higher ground as my mother assured me we would find the perfect dry cleaner to make it like new once again. In my exhaustion, I tried to disengage from the last twenty-four hours that seemed like a nightmare.

The wedding that I had looked forward to all of my life now seemed threatened—not merely because of a stain on the bottom edges of my beautiful wedding dress, but because of the threatening, permanent medical stain that could make my fiancé change his mind about marrying me. I kept thinking that this was a terrible way to start our marriage. The man I loved had not yet committed to any vow of "for better or for worse, in sickness or in health". I knew that he must be given the chance to be released from his commitment to marry me.

CHAPTER TWO
SEEING BEYOND COMMITMENT

All my life I had longed for a godly man who would love the Lord and lead His people. From the first time I was introduced to Tony McWilliams, I was attracted to his singleness of vision and principled living. He was tall and handsome with blue penetrating eyes just for me. He had a way of opening a passage of scripture and helping others to see more clearly. I gladly was his attentive student and biggest fan. We complemented each other because he was the quiet, unshakable anchor, and I was the social, excitable type who jumped with her heart. We both were passionate communicators concerning the gospel. He was the constant and ever-stable rock that I always needed. Only God could have arranged for a Missouri girl and Southern Illinois boy to meet in Florida as we worked side by side in a ministry.

It had seemed like an eternity since that special night when Tony proposed by saying, "I want to spend the rest of my life serving God with you." From the first moment that we sensed our friendship deepening, we knelt to surrender our lives and desires to Him. We declared together in prayer, "Jesus, be the Lord of our relationship."

Tony and I were married on the most romantic day of the year—April 15, income tax day. Though we may have been shortsighted, not knowing we would feel the pressure of having to pay the government on our anniversaries, we still knew that our wedding was to be in the springtime.

My brother and sister were living in Jerusalem, Israel, at the time. Jon was attending the Hebrew University for a year, and Candy was working at the Garden Tomb. Our wedding date fell perfectly in the middle of spring break, enabling both of them to come home. I was in awe of God's precise planning and provision long before we even knew to ask Him.

Tony and I had written our wedding invitation and vows because we wanted to personally express our commitment to the Savior who had brought our lives together. After all, we knew from the scriptures that Jesus was accustomed to going to weddings; they state that He helped at the marriage reception of his friend. He had been invited to ours, as well.

The day was beautiful and people came from everywhere. The music was orchestrated to begin promptly one hour before the processional. I had carefully picked all the music with each minute timed perfectly. However, at two o'clock when the ceremony was about to begin, people stood at the door of the church and lined the sidewalk. I was disappointed that my perfect timing had gone awry. The signing of the guest book had held up the seating, so it was promptly closed and the groomsmen and ushers were sent outside to help get the people seated as quickly as possible.

I stood in a back room by my dad's side, watching people scurry around. One of the ushers had escorted my maternal grandmother to a seat one row behind the family. A space hadn't been saved for her, and he didn't want everyone to have to move down a seat. As he walked down the aisle, I caught his eye and motioned for him to go back and seat her with the other grandparents. Without hesitation, he twirled around and asked for my grandmother's arm once again. I am sure that my Grandmother, already feeling slighted to be behind the other family members, now thought she was being escorted out of the church instead of being advanced one row. As the usher and my elderly grandmother stood looking at the crowded row, he was perplexed as to how to seat her. He lifted both hands like a choral director signaling everyone in the family section to rise to their feet. I watched as a row of elderly loved ones looked on in confusion. I was only grateful they did not break out in song as the usher tried to conduct his senior choir. Finally, Grandmother was seated, along with the rest of the waiting crowd.

The short delay was quickly forgotten as the ceremony began. Earlier, when my husband walked out with his attendants, he caught his breath as he felt a holy presence sweep over the audience. He knew, indeed, that the Lord had come to witness our covenant exchange.

The church had a two-story sanctuary with a curved balcony that had a stairway. My graceful bridesmaids looked beautiful descending the steps while worship music filled the air. Tony's distinguished groomsmen awaited each lady at the foot of the steps and escorted them to their honored places.

At last, it was time for my walk down the aisle with my father. I had always said that I would never cry at my own wedding. Too much emotion was needless energy. It could also ruin my makeup. The minute we stepped out from the back room, I began to weep as I, too, caught my breath in wonderment. We did not walk alone.

After a few steps, my Dad looked at me and whispered, "You don't have to do this if you don't want to." I will always love him for that tender moment when he wanted to make sure my decision was firm regardless of the wedding expense and planning. However, I was unmoved, and my decision stood. In only a few moments I would be committed to the handpicked man of God who waited patiently for me.

Our dear friend and senior pastor received us at the altar and then my dad performed the rest of the service. Our wedding included communion administered by our fathers along with their spoken blessing over us. Tony's vows were filled with scriptures, and my vows were sung to my new husband. After the nuptial charge had been given to Tony and me, we turned to our audience and challenged them with the gospel. Tony spoke and I sang. Our separate ministries had come together for our first gathering. A word of exhortation came that day saying to us, "Go, for my people are waiting."

We sealed our commitment with a kiss, and we swiftly walked down the aisle to a joyful song. We had taken the challenge to "Go, for His people were waiting."

People were waiting all right—in our long reception line. The line was so long that we later heard of one woman who, while waiting in line, decided to run to the grocery store to do her shopping and then returned to stand in line once more. It was a delight to greet everyone and receive their prayers and good wishes. God had moved among the congregation. We heard testimonies of all kinds from people in the line who had given their hearts to the Lord. Others found a new freedom to walk in Christ.

As an act of kindness we had predetermined to take our wedding pictures after our guests had begun to eat at the reception. Not taking our pictures before greeting our guests was a BIG mistake. All the hugging in the reception line had rumpled our hair and our wedding attire and had smashed our flowers. When we finally returned to the empty sanctuary to take our wedding pictures, we were shocked. The janitor had put the church furniture back in place and the florist had taken all of the beautiful flowers, even though we had purchased them. To this day my mom still considers this a sore subject, and I cannot help but wonder if the floral arrangements disappeared to the nearest funeral home. Instead of flowers for a backdrop, our wedding pictures have church flags.

After good wishes and prayers with long hugs, we departed on our journey as man and wife. Our honeymoon was peaceful in Paris—Paris, Tennessee, that is. One minister that Tony often traveled with had given us advice before we married, saying, "Tell people not to call you while you are on your honeymoon. Instead, say you will call them." Great advice. However, he was the first to call us six days into our honeymoon. He asked Tony to come teach at a Bible school because they had a last-minute cancellation. We remembered Jesus' words: "Go, for my people are waiting" —and we went.

CHAPTER THREE
SEEING BEYOND
THE MORNING

Before our marriage we both had been crisscrossing the country with our single ministries. After our wedding, our lifestyle remained the same, with "constant going" for the next year. Our desire was to purchase a travel trailer to use as our home on the road. God had provided a new van before we were married, and its engine was perfect for pulling a trailer. However, the price tag for a trailer seemed huge for newlyweds with modest love offerings from churches. In spite of our limited cash flow, we knew that He was more than enough. We prayed and asked God to lead us.

One day in Illinois, my dad saw a trailer sitting on a used-RV lot that was three blocks from my parent's house. It had just arrived and was one of the top models, in mint condition. God had positioned it right in front of our eyes. When we walked through the entire twenty-nine feet of mobile home, we fell in love with it. It was exactly what we had asked the Lord to provide. Acquiring the amount for the trailer seemed impossible, but God was interested in our trusting Him. So, we committed to pray.

Soon thereafter, on a Wednesday evening at church, the treasurer told us that someone had given an anonymous donation to our ministry. Smiling, she handed us a check for the exact amount of the trailer, insurance, and license tag, with fifty dollars left over.

We had underestimated His commitment to supply all that would be needed for us to "Go".

That trailer was our only home for over six months, but in December, we parked our travel trailer beside a house with a foundation. We rented a small three bedroom home, and we lived near my parents, just outside the city where we were married. The small town provided a good base for our ministry, but the name of the town required a vivid imagination because it meant "fat hill." In reality, nothing but fertile, flat fields of corn and soybeans surrounded this community. I loved being able to set up more permanent housekeeping and using the trailer only for ministry trips.

A few days before Christmas, snow covered the ground, making a picturesque landscape. A small, modest tree with borrowed ornaments sat in front of the picture window with three priceless gifts under it. My husband had surprised me with a beautiful Tiffany lamp before the holidays. It was our first treasured piece of furniture, in addition to a new wooden rocker that I loved. My cozy, favorite corner was now complete. Our possessions were scarce, yet we were wealthy beyond words because we had each other.

I was busy with preparations and cleaning because we were expecting special holiday guests. My parents were in Israel visiting my sister who was still working at the Garden Tomb in Jerusalem. They had gone to enjoy the holidays with her as well as to help her move into a new apartment. I smiled to think how special all of our holidays would be—Tony's and my first Christmas together in our own house, and my parents' and sister's in Bethlehem on Christmas Eve .

It seemed strange, though, for my family to not be together for the holidays. Oh, how I missed them. My brother came from the University of Illinois where he studied law, and having him with us was a familiar source of joy and comfort. Since my mother was away, I attempted to fill her role by baking Jon's favorite snowball cookies, and I watched with great satisfaction as he devoured them all.

Another "first" for me was cooking for the holidays and our special houseguests. Having the role as first lady of my own home permitted me to embrace hospitality and all the work that comes with it. I was still getting used to all of it, not to mention adapting to being a daughter-in-law. Tony's parents drove from southern Illinois to be our company for the first time. Among our guests, the most enthusiastic of all was Tony's little sister, Cathy, who was fifteen years younger than he. The little curly-haired seven-year old jumped with anticipation, and her excitement was contagious.

Tony's family planned to leave early Christmas morning. My husband was breaking tradition by not going to his grandparent's farm with all the extended family for Christmas Day, choosing, instead, to be in his own home. We were at the threshold of many new beginnings and the making of our own memories. Also, we were going to be traveling on the day after Christmas and needed time to prepare and pack.

Our unexpected event early Christmas morning confirmed that we had made the right choice. When I went to bed on Christmas Eve I lay down worn out from all of the activities of the week. We had given our bedroom to my husband's parents and the spare bedroom to my brother. Tony's sister slept on the floor in her parent's room. We had made a bed for ourselves on the living room floor under our humble Christmas tree. Tony's family planned to leave at sunrise and eat breakfast on the road. I appreciated their being low maintenance, since I was exhausted.

I awoke when I heard others, and I moved from our bed on the floor over to my new rocker by crawling, since it was near our makeshift pallet. No one watching would have thought this was odd since there were suitcases and empty boxes to maneuver around from the family gathering the previous night. Tony's parents lingered to visit for a short moment, much to my young sister-in-law's disappointment. She was focused on the day before her and the goodies that awaited her at Grandmother's house. I, too, was anxious for them to leave. Finally, we exchanged goodbyes and holiday wishes, and then they were on their way.

When I think about that morning, I wonder how I managed to give the greatest performance of my life. Upon opening my eyes minutes previously I knew that something was drastically wrong. However, I didn't want to alarm anyone and I knew that my husband and I would be alone in moments. So, I decided to fake my way through a normal goodbye—but it was anything but normal. I had awakened on Christmas Day with no eyesight. Everything was black.

Just the night before I had had perfect 20/20 vision. Obviously, this was the forewarning that the research medical team had given to me. I had quickly suppressed that haunting report about my eyes before I was married, but I think even the doctors didn't believe it would happen so quickly. How do you prepare for having perfect eyesight one day and blindness the next? I thought that, if any visual impairment happened, it would occur gradually and a new medical breakthrough would be offered along the way. No one could have prepared me for this rude interruption and grief. What had happened?

As soon as Tony's parents left, I cried out, alarmed and in shock, to my husband, "I can't see!" I began to cry and tell him how afraid I was. What a terrible first Christmas gift to give to the man of my dreams. Our world had forever dreadfully changed sometime in the night.

My husband held me as I wept in disbelief and fear. We were to leave the following morning for a trip to the Southwest with other young adults, including my brother. Tony and I were scheduled to speak at a youth rally in Pasadena, Texas, and I also was the guest musical artist for a concert on New Year's Eve.

Since the eye specialists we needed were not available because of the holidays, our focus remained on leaving for Texas with a purpose in front of us. I asked my husband, "How will we go? What will I do?" He held me and said that God would be our helper. I remember his direct words of leadership to this fallen soldier. "This is not a time to retreat." I lay on the bed as my husband and brother prayed over me.

I remember little about that cold, snowy day except for being held by my husband. He never mentioned his fears or anger for this disruption in our lives. I wondered if he saw the long road in front of him and the uncertain days with the wife of his youth, or did he have only enough strength for the moment? Neither of us had planned on our vows of loving each other "for better or worse, in sickness and health" being challenged so quickly.

I vividly do remember, however, getting a phone call from my parents in Israel that Christmas Day. They kept asking if we were all right. I never told them of our new battle because I wanted to protect them. Besides, they were too far away to do anything except worry. I had never considered that they were already praying. My dad said later that God had forewarned him that something was wrong with us, and that is why he kept asking if we were all right. I underestimated the loving concern and sensitivity of parents who heard from God and who had been my spiritual covering all of my life. I felt so alone. Our common bond and tie was Bethlehem. My mind and heart set its gaze on the last stanza of the Christmas hymn,

"O Little Town of Bethlehem…The hopes and fears of all the years are met in Thee tonight."

I called a young friend asking if she would be able to accompany us to the youth rally and assist me. Asking for help was a humbling road beyond words, especially because I was skilled in my independence. I asked if she would be my eyes on the trip and help me with my wardrobe and hair. My newly appointed personal assistant agreed to aid me. As I prepared to leave on the ministry trip, I was determined not to retreat, in spite of being stricken with blindness. Grace alone and His incomprehensible strength counteracted my weakness. Learning to depend on the Savior and others would become my lifetime lesson. I felt the pressure to learn it quickly in order to survive.

I marvel over our continuing on with our planned ministry engagement. This would be the pattern for our lives, modeled in each storm that lay ahead. The only way to redeem the fight and battle was to see His kingdom advanced. "In our weakness He is made strong" became more than an ornate wall-hanging in our home. It now was about to be tested. From afar, I had admired my heroes of faith who had faced their own adversities. However, now I embraced them as fellow comrades who stood looking over the balcony of heaven cheering, "Don't retreat." Like them, I was also in need of a Savior who was ever present to help in my trouble.

I am grateful for a husband of great inner strength who focused on the answer to our crisis and not just the details of our storm. He has always been a rock of unwavering courage, setting his heart on responding and not merely reacting. He has helped quiet me in the storms that have attempted to capsize us in life. We both have anchored our lives on the rock of our salvation—Jesus Christ alone has been the stabilizing factor, saying calmly, "Peace. Peace."

The day after Christmas we set out on our trip to Texas. I remember little of the trip and its difficult changes. Besides handling my blindness, my concern was also what I would say to those whom I would meet. I anticipated their shock at seeing my immediate deterioration and my vain attempt to explain something I did not yet understand myself. Along with my own battles, I have always tried to carry everyone else's. I have also felt the need to protect God and His reputation. I did not want others to question the goodness of God and His ability based on my life. I have always known that my actions represent Him. Often, the load of carrying others while trying to be strong for myself has been an unnecessary burden and needless load. God is well able to defend Himself. His character and ability is unchangeable and proven since the beginning of time. Nevertheless, trying to protect Him became one of the driving factors of my life as I walked through storms while a host of people watched from the sidelines.

The youth rally was no different. People watched as I learned to maneuver in the dark. I taught some workshops and mingled with the young people, but I struggled with not being able to move around independently. I was constantly in the presence of someone else. My husband's arm became my dearest friend. As a couple, we were adjusting to this awkward new dance of suffering. I told him that if he would simply offer his arm to me, no one would have to know that I was blind. He would look like a perfect gentlemen and I would look like his treasured lady. Though there were triumphant moments in the middle of the uncertainty, I privately wrestled through tears, anger and disappointment. I was aware that my heart would not let me fully grieve due to the required performance I had demanded of myself. Surely, this trial would leave as quickly as it came.

I wondered which doctor I would call first when we returned home. I questioned if I should see any specialists while in the Houston area, as the city offered a wider range of excellent medical choices. I did not know what to do or where to turn. Tony and I only talked about the answers and verses we had put to memory that comforted us. We could not afford anything less than faith in a God who could do the impossible. The fight to simply survive took all of my energy.

The concert came at the end of the rally. My part of the program was to be followed by communion and then prayer as we all welcomed the New Year in together. Up until that time, I routinely ended each concert with a song that now was my deepest heart's cry, "Open my eyes, Lord; I want to see Jesus." The song became a penetrating cry of my audience, also, for they had been watching my every move during the rally and they were heartsick, too. Tears flowed down the cheeks of many.

Surprisingly, during the song I began to see some light. Before that time everything seemed black with no clarity of sight. I was ecstatic and full of anticipation. I knew that one glimpse of light inspired me to hope for more. I clung to the One who would bring joy in the morning after the long nights of sorrow. I would learn to trust Him. My continual cry remained, "Open my eyes, Lord."

On New Year's Day we began our journey back to the Midwest. With each hour the darkness seemed to be lifting, and I could see some things. Later, I learned that the blood vessels behind both of my eyes had hemorrhaged and my eyes were sitting in their own pools of blood. What had brought about this sudden change?

CHAPTER FOUR
SEEING BEYOND THE NEWS

It seems as if all of my life I have been monitored by some kind of doctor or medical consultant. For the most part, the counsel and instructions from everyone in white coats conditioned my heart to simply endure the visits. I mostly viewed each checkup as regular maintenance that interrupted one more day of living. I always saw the doctors as a deterrent to the dreams and hopes I had for my life. My survival mechanisms kept me from hearing their negative predictions that lacked hope.

However, there was one day when the doctor's words invaded my soul with fear. That day, the doctor stood as my judge to sentence me with two verdicts. He declared at what age I would probably die and proclaimed that I would never be a mother. I have since learned that doctors simply "practice" medicine, and they sometimes get it wrong.

I can remember the doctor's face when he was telling me my future as he saw it. He told me that I would most likely never have children, due to my childhood disease. Also, he thought it would be a good idea if I did something more with my life than just music, because, he said, "I don't want you to be a fat, gospel pianist." I wondered which was the joke and what was the truth? I remember being sad over the possibility of not experiencing motherhood; however, as a young invincible teen, that pain was not much of a threat because my future seemed so bright. I left his office that day with a focus on living my life to the fullest. Whatever difficulties awaited me would be taken care of then. For now, I had too much to do.

Shortly after I married Tony, I loudly heard the doctor's decree in my head, threatening my hopes for a family. The doctors' words from the past were now running like recordings in my mind. But Tony and I still longed for children. We had seen the promise and potential of a household who declared Christ as Lord. We knew that every good and perfect gift came from the Father, and this included children. Our lives were committed to serving Him, and we wanted all that heaven offered.

I remember reading the Bible one day as a young girl and seeing the heart of God. I read that what He desired were godly offspring. I had seen the effects of telling His story from generation to generation throughout the Bible. Children were more than an inconvenience and financial drain; they were assets. Psalm 127 compares children to arrows in the hands of a mighty warrior. While my vision for family increased, my hopes were diminished, especially since I'd found myself with impaired vision from that black Christmas morning. As my eyesight returned, I was aware that some damage had taken place. My clarity of vision was not as keen, and it was more difficult to read regular print. Before this change, I had been the one who others said had eagle vision. I was the first to see the farthest signs along the road as well as items that others overlooked. I had never even needed glasses. Now there were no glasses that could help. I feared losing my driver's license that embodied my independence. With troubling concern, I dreamt of children who would depend on me. Who would chauffeur them? It was too much to figure out in my mind, so I simply resolved to trust the God who could do the impossible while also granting my heart's desire.

At this time, I had a close friend who also wanted a baby. She and her husband had chosen to work in their careers before having children, but now they were anxious for a child. One day my friend Ann called; she was overjoyed to tell me that she was pregnant. Though I was happy for her, I reminded her that we had prayed we would be pregnant together. My emotions were mixed as I hung up the phone, hearing once again the doctor's voice telling me I would probably never have children.

To my great delight and surprise, I, too, discovered that I was pregnant weeks later. The doctors were wrong. I could have a baby, after all. Our due date was in the summer, and I shared the joyous news with Ann. We grew in friendship and belly, and our babies were born four days apart.

At the time, we were living in a town of nearly 100,000 people in central Illinois. I had never been told that I would need a specialist trained in diabetic pregnancies if I were to conceive and bear a child. Innocently ignorant, we had found and secured an elderly obstetrician. He never ordered special tests except for some periodic blood work at the hospital. My doctor visits were routine although nearly four months into my pregnancy I had been hospitalized to monitor my blood sugar levels more closely. The doctor had thought that I might need some adjustments with my insulin dosages as the baby developed, so he consulted another physician about me. I was perplexed as to why I was being hospitalized at the same time my doctor was leaving on vacation.

The nurses delivered the doctor's request for me to exercise while I stayed in the hospital for a few days. My only outlets were to walk the stairwells and the halls of the hospital floor. A membership to the local athletic club could have served me better than this hospital visit. Later, I was told that the nurses had recorded me as being hyperactive and always on the move. Looking back, my medical case was as haphazard as a Laurel and Hardy movie minus the laughter.

My eyes had not worsened, but now the mystery of the Christmas morning hemorrhaging had been solved. It was due to pregnancy. The hormonal changes mixed with the dynamics of fluctuating blood sugar levels caused the eye vessels to break and bleed. In our family, the gift of life would come at a high price.

On Monday afternoon, August 27th, I went to the doctor for my weekly exam. I was nearly full-term and fully in bloom with new life. Upon my visit, the doctor discovered my blood pressure to be unacceptably high, and I was ordered to go directly to the hospital. He said he did not even want me to go home to gather my things. He instructed me to immediately check myself into the hospital, and he would call ahead with orders. I followed his request, and within the hour I was lying in a hospital gown preparing myself for the birth of our first child.

At once, the staff connected me to a fetal monitor and hooked an IV to my arm in order to start my contractions. I panicked trying to remember the stages of our Lamaze training. I certainly was not ready for the sudden hard pains of contractions without any natural, gradual increase. After two long hours, the doctor finally arrived to check on me. At one glance, he noticed that the monitor was not even working. With angry profanities, he quickly demanded a change in machines. Within minutes it showed that our child was in distress. The doctor, visibly irritated, told the nurses to prepare me for surgery. I was too miserable to be upset. While I was being prepped, the doctor asked if I wanted my appendix. Somewhat distracted by the cold hands on my belly and the scurry of nurses working on me, I asked, "Do I need it?" He promptly replied, "No, so I will take it out." I was out of control as things moved quickly all around me. I could only think of our son who was about to be born.

We had never seen the gender of the baby we were carrying by way of sonogram, but others convinced me it was a boy. I remember the staff wearing pink scrubs and caps as they rolled me into surgery. I told them they had picked out the wrong color from their wardrobe because we were about to give birth to a baby boy. It was now 8:00 at night and the day was a blur.

The doctor had strongly suggested that I have a spinal block so I would be alert through the Cesarean procedure. My initial wish was to be put to sleep and then awaken with a new bundle of baby in my arms. However, the doctor had gotten his way on every other decision up to now, and I was at his mercy and judgment.

The group of caregivers went to work manning their posts as they fulfilled their own responsibilities on this life-giving team. The anesthesiologist said that my feet and legs would feel warm at first and then soon afterward my stomach would be numb so I would not feel any part of the knife. This was indeed comforting. My only problem was that I could feel the medicine as it started from my feet and gradually moved up my body to my neck.

Strapped to the table with an oxygen mask on, along with other important monitoring machines and wires, I nervously asked, "Hey. Is this numb feeling supposed to be up to my throat?" No one answered me, but I heard the sounds of many feet moving fast around the room. "Jesus," I cried, "keep us safe!" The tension was mounting in the room, and my scar testifies to the swiftness of the surgeon's knife. He cut me open from the naval down like a watermelon at a church picnic.

In minutes, someone told me that our baby was a little girl. I kept saying in my oxygen mask, "Girl. A girl? Oh God, thank you for a girl. A girl! Our girl!" I was shocked but finally felt that I could breathe again with new room for my lungs to expand. Alarmingly, there was something missing. I had heard no sounds from my baby girl. At last there was a small whimper with a bit of a cry.

"Is my baby all right?" I asked. No one answered me. I asked once more. Quickly, a nurse swept by me with my little girl, but I was only able to hear a faint noise and catch a glimpse of her thick black hair. Anna Gail McWilliams had arrived at last. I lay on the table for nearly an hour while they sewed my stomach back together and as I praised God for our daughter. I kept saying over and over, "A little girl. I can hardly believe it!"

The worst was over—or was it?

CHAPTER FIVE
SEEING BEYOND THE CRISIS

Little did I know that the only time I would see my baby daughter during the next several days would be that passing glance when the nurse rushed past. Our daughter was very sick. Every minute counted in this fight for her life.

Anna weighed nine pounds and nine ounces, but much of it was unhealthy fluid buildup. Years later we were to discover that diabetic pregnancies rarely go full term as we had done. Not only was her life in danger, but so was mine.

Tony had not been allowed to accompany me into the surgery room to see Anna's birth, because it was considered an emergency. He paced the floor praying as he waited for some news.

An attending nurse brought the news bulletin of Anna's birth to Tony in the father's waiting lounge. However, they also informed him that Anna would have to be closely observed during the night, but failed to provide any real details. We were encouraged to focus on my recovery. It was not until the next morning that we were told the truth. Anna was in crisis.

Once in the recovery room, I wanted to call everyone on my list of special family and friends. My first call was to my parents. Not only were they awaiting the news, but also the Bible Study group of young women who were meeting there eagerly waited for the reports. For years, the group had affectionately been called the

"Monday Night Girlie Meeting." My mother led the group that met in my parents' home. I was part of the group, and during the years we had met together we had watched our lives develop in God and His ways. Our prayers for one another had also produced answers to our hearts' cries for husbands, children, jobs, and other pressing needs. It seemed appropriate to know that the Monday night girlies were praying for me to be delivered.

I next called my sister in Israel. It was during this conversation that the nurse came and grabbed the phone out of my hands. With a mean tone of voice, she said, "You are not to talk to anyone. Your life is in danger." She quickly ushered my husband out of the room, closed the door, and flipped off the lights. "Can anyone tell me what is happening?" I was left alone to wonder.

The next person permitted to enter the room was a drill sergeant nurse from some war zone. She began pressing down on my abdomen to check if my uterus was contracting. At that point, I knew that I had been short-changed in the amount of drugs I was given in surgery. In spite of my large incision, I nearly came off of the bed to flatten that nurse. No wonder my blood pressure was sky-high. "Bring back my husband," became my demand now. I needed someone to stand in the gap, not only to pray for me but also to protect me from that cruel nurse. My blood pressure had reached extremely dangerous levels, and they feared for my life.

We did not realize that only a few doors down the hall our baby lay desperately fighting for every breath she took. Our hospital was not equipped to handle a high-risk trauma with an infant. The staff had immediately placed Anna under unnecessarily large amounts of oxygen. They also gave her a heart medication to race her heart when, in reality, she needed the opposite—something to calm her heart.

Due to my diabetic condition, Anna's pancreas had been working overtime to take care of her needs and help with mine. This made the umbilical cord a lifeline that we extended to each other. I offered her life while she tried to offer me something I desperately needed—insulin. This caused her pancreas to be over stimulated since mine was not working at all. Consequently, when she was born her pancreas kept functioning at the same heightened level, causing her blood sugar to be dangerously low. Glucose was quickly pumped into her system, as the medical team marveled that she was not already in a coma. While the Great Physician alone held her life in His hands, the doctors tried to solve her complicated problems. Time was of the essence.

Eventually, Tony was permitted to return to my side. When I slept, Tony slipped out to catch a glimpse of his little girl. When he finally located her in a private room empty of other newborns, he peeked through the cracks of the closed blinds of the nursery window. Painfully, he watched as Anna was laboring to breathe. Nurses and doctors surrounded her as they rapidly worked to stabilize her condition. Tony looked on with a deepening concern for his new charge. The seriousness of the situation at this late hour was obvious—both of Tony's ladies were in trouble.

It had been twenty-four hours since I had become the mother of our firstborn daughter, Anna. I kept asking the nurses when I could see her, but I was always given some excuse. Nurses insisted that I needed rest and so did Anna. During that first twenty-four hours my blood pressure had finally stabilized. Though a new level of physical pain had begun, nothing compared to the growing pain of my heart. I had given birth to a child that I had never held or touched. When would I see my baby and hold her?

It was late at night and I was alone. I knew that all the tests had confirmed the obvious—Anna was a very sick baby with little or no hope of survival. I had agonized as nurses brought my roommate her new bundle of life every three hours for feeding while I longed for my own. I was in no condition to walk down to the nursery by myself after having had my stomach cut open and still feeling the effects of surgery.

Each hour someone brought an updated report about my daughter's condition. Ironically, a visually impaired physician had been called onto the case for consultation. He insisted that the hospital transport Anna to the high-risk center immediately. His persistence saved our daughter's life. Tony delivered the news that our firstborn would be transferred to another city in hopes of helping her. Would I ever hold her? My heart was torn, and I feared letting her go. I pleaded to be allowed to see her and pray over her before she began her journey by ambulance. The doctors agreed that once Anna was placed in her isolette—ready, and packed for the journey—I could tell her goodbye. We learned later that the staff thought it would be our final goodbye.

The hospital provided a private room for Tony and me, along with my parents who had joined us for prayer. My husband wheeled me into the room where we sat waiting for our baby. Our moments were to be short, for her life hung in the balance. Just before they brought Anna to us, my obstetrician poked his head in the door to give us his condolences and sympathy. He was beginning to prepare her death certificate. I, on the other hand, was focused on the Giver of Life.

Finally, our treasure arrived. Our small private room filled with emotion. We all began to weep as we cried out to the Lord in prayer. I reached inside the isolette, longing to touch my little one. I began to talk to her as I rubbed the open palm of her newborn hand with my finger. I told her that I was her mommy and I loved her. I then told her to fight for life, reassuring her that we would be together again soon. She clasped my finger, and I heard the Lord speak deep in my spirit, "Just as she is holding on to you, hold on to Me!" Through tears of brokenness, we committed our firstborn into His care. Silence fell on us as Anna was wheeled out to her life-care ride while I was wheeled back to my room to weep. We were soon to learn that her ride would be hijacked by an encounter with death.

Within minutes of leaving the local hospital, the experienced medical rescue team removed Anna's oxygen, allowing her to breathe on her own. The dangerously high amounts of oxygen she had previously been given in the hospital had threatened her eyesight, as well as her hearing. In addition, the mistaken heart medication given to her earlier could have killed her. In spite of constant care during the transport, Anna died. The medical team managed to revive her. It was apparent that the Great Physician rode with her as the team frantically worked to preserve her young life.

After Tony had made sure I was settled, he left to follow the ambulance. I was forced to stay behind in the hospital where I had delivered my daughter. My lowest point of coping was when the babies were rolled out to visit their mommies for feeding times. As my strength was restored and I could walk again, I would stand in the hallway every time my roommate's baby was brought to her. I wrestled with thoughts of injustice. I wondered, "Who was holding mine?"

CHAPTER SIX
SEEING BEYOND
FAREWELL

Late one night, my dad came alone to my hospital room to take my husband's place. He had always been the strong defender in my life and it hurt him to see that he could not fix my pain. He bent over and softly asked how I was doing. Inconsolably, I cried, "Dad, if I lose her, then you will lose me."

As I weaved in and out of hope and despair, a friend was preaching at a Christian convention in a neighboring state. During the service, he had been handed a note telling of our crisis. He immediately stopped the meeting and asked the hundreds in attendance to pray for our daughter. I will always be grateful for his act of loving kindness. Prayer was our lifeline.

Across town at another hospital, my friend, Ann, delivered her first son in the middle of my crisis. The nurses' station received a call for me after hours, and a night nurse slipped into my room at midnight to give me the news that my friend was a new mommy and all was well. Our prayers had been answered about having our babies at the same time. I wept into my pillow after hearing that hers was perfectly fine while knowing that mine was so sick. All of the pain medicine I was taking to ease my discomfort could not ease the pain of my questioning heart. What had gone wrong?

People react and respond to tragedy in strange and different ways. Some had answers to questions I had not even asked. Others were afraid to visit because they didn't know what to say. Still others expressed their love by sending the flowers and gifts that now filled my room. A few tried to distract me, unsuccessfully, with their own stories of medical heartache. Many just came to sit and ask if I was all right. One dear lady on staff at the church where we were married came every day to pray for me and console me. Often, I found myself counseling others on the phone when they would call about Anna. Though they had called to comfort me, they would inevitably break down and cry when they heard the story. Still, some were just insensitive. One visitor was a clamorous girl who was new to our weekly Bible study. Her opening remarks were, "I have a gift for Anna, but I wanted to see if she's going to live first." I refused to spend extra energy on anything but reaching for the Great Physician's coat and asking Him for a miracle. I could not afford any stumbling blocks because too much was at stake.

I was determined to find a way to escape the hospital in order to follow Anna and be with her. During my stay I had made many friends, one very special one being my morning nurse. I asked her if she would notify me each new dawn when my doctor arrived in the building so I could put my plan into action. The doctor's routine was to make early morning rounds, and the two of us had the time of his arrival marked. I would quickly style my hair, apply makeup, and stand at the foot of my bed, anticipating his arrival. When he finally entered my room, my strategy was to ask him first, "How are you today?" so I could stay in control. He remarked how amazed he was that I seemed to be recovering so quickly. My doctor never had a clue that I collapsed back on the bed in pain after he would leave the room. My award-winning acting eventually won my release.

The next four days turned into a test as I focused only on being released from the hospital to move to where my daughter was. I wanted free of my prison. I wanted to be with my daughter. She needed me, and I needed her.

Resolutely, I persisted, "Doctor, may I please go home?" He, surprisingly, inquired, "Are you sure you are ready to go?" I was aware that he was leaving for a four-day vacation out of state, so I knew my release must be swift or otherwise I could be stuck. We stood staring at each other, neither of us willing to yield ground. The doctor hesitantly said that I could leave the hospital if I promised to go straight home to rest. I was tempted to lie for one second, but then knew that I must tell the truth. "No, doctor! I am leaving here to go be with my little girl. She needs me!" Scowling in disapproval, he stood pondering my words, tempted to exercise his control over me by demanding that I not be released from his care. Without missing a minute of negotiating strategy, I quickly added that my game plan was for my husband and me to check into a motel across the street from the neonatal center. There we would be able to monitor Anna's progress, and I could rest as often as I needed to. The doctor stood in my doorway, perplexed and indecisive for a moment, but he then agreed to my plan. I breathed a deep sigh of relief as he walked away to finish his written report and fill out the release papers. At last I was free. I knew that I would need every ounce of energy that I could muster to face the winding road that now lay in front of me. A baby was waiting for her mommy.

I called Tony and asked him to come quickly before the doctors had a chance to change their minds. I requested a pain pill before I began packing my belongings as I prepared to go to the neonatal high-risk unit in a city forty-five miles away. I had one stop to make first before leaving.

My husband agreed to take me to another hospital across town to see my friend, Ann. I knew that I might not be coming home for a long time. It was painful to imagine that our dream of having babies together had now turned into a nightmare for me. I was uncertain how I would react to see a healthy baby in the arms of my friend while mine lay with life support tubes throughout her body. Nevertheless, I knew that I wanted to congratulate her.

Tony dropped me off at the front entrance to the hospital. While Tony parked the car, I decided to wait for him inside. As soon as I walked through the sliding doors, two volunteers rushed to offer me a wheelchair. I was surprised at their prompt attention and presumption that I needed their services. They told me that they saw the hospital band on my arm and I looked distraught and pale. Obviously, my pregnant-looking figure had not changed much in four days. I was tempted to accept their offer since my morning pain pill was wearing off; however, I declined the ride and chose to walk.

In silence, Tony and I rode the elevator to locate Ann with her firstborn. Our eyes met as we greeted each other. Hers were filled with joy over a nearly perfect birth experience, while mine filled with the pain of arms that were still empty and the dread of what may lie down the road. We embraced one another as she whispered, "I am so sorry," and as I whispered at the same time, "I am so happy for you." It now seemed as if a swift, raging river separated my dear friend and me, with her being on one side and me on the other. Our embrace would be a farewell...for a season.

CHAPTER SEVEN
SEEING BEYOND
HOPELESSNESS

At last, I was on my way to stand by the side of our infant soldier. One thing we knew: the battle was the Lord's. No one from the medical community had expected Anna to live. I do not remember talking to Tony during the hour trip, but our cries to God were constant. We checked into the motel directly across from the neonatal center, not realizing that we would live there for the next twenty-one days. My sole reason for coming was to be with my daughter to help her fight for her life.

It was evening by the time I first entered the high-risk unit. There were six levels of nurseries, rated by the severity of the children. Anna lay in Preemie One, the most critical of all. Eight other babies close to death shared the room. I could not stop the tears when I saw my little one fighting for every labored breath. She was on her back with tubes connected to her arms, legs, and head. Because of the tubes, they had shaved some of her beautiful thick, dark hair on the sides of her head, making her look as if she had a bad Mohawk haircut. Already, many of her veins had collapsed. She wore patches of cotton taped over her eyes to protect them from the bright lights combating her high level of jaundice. The soles of her feet were black and blue from nurses drawing blood from them every two hours. Her abdomen was distended and her breathing rapid. I bent over her isolette and whispered, "Anna, Mommy is here to help you fight. Live my little one. Live."

We had to scrub our hands and put on gowns, masks, and hairnets before staff permitted us near our infant daughter. God was good to cover us with grace as we absorbed the shock of the condition of our baby. The surrounding heart monitors seemed to beat in rhythm as every heart rate and pulse were being watched by skillful teams of physicians. My arms longed to hold Anna, but I knew she must remain unmoved as she now rested under the Great Physician's care. He was near and had heard our cries.

When we were not with Anna for the few moments of visitation, we would sit in the waiting room with other troubled parents who waited for a word of hope. I, like most of the other parents, did not want to carry on any shallow conversation for we all were distracted from the routine of our normal lives. Nothing interested me except the wellbeing of our daughter.

One night, I vividly remember our walking down the hall to enter Preemie One. A dark heaviness filled the air and sent cold shivers down my back. I breathed deeply, fearing what faced us at the end of the hallway. The background noise of heart monitors beeping and ventilators running created a symphony of sounds that disquieted the hearts of waiting parents, sending many to their knees. I knew that we all needed a healing Savior. After only moments of standing near our daughter, the nurses ushered us out of the room as quickly as we had entered. Within the hour, every baby in that Critical Care Preemie Unit had died, except Anna. The Death Angel had been present, stealing away his victims in the night without permission. When I returned to Anna's side, I declard over her, Psalm 118, verse 17: "You will live and not die and declare what God has done forever."

From the very start of the battle, I wrestled with a decision that I had to make. Everything around me looked hopeless, and the doctors never gave us any reason to hope. I scrambled to find a solid place on which to stand as I braced myself for this new, unexpected battle. I was well aware that the outcome could be death. My final recollection was to focus on what Job of the scriptures said, "Though you slay me, yet I will trust You." I was confident that He alone could be trusted, and His grace would enable me to stand, no matter what the result. However, my vision was set on fighting while Anna had breath. The battle would not be over until then. Once again, the Word of God became my survival manual. I was comforted, as well as encouraged, by Ephesians 6:13, "Having done all—stand." I anchored my feet on the side of life.

It is in the heart of any battle that the hope and life-giving counsel of the Bible become clear. The Psalms calmed me when I read, "The Lord is my light and my salvation; whom shall I fear? The Lord is the strength of my heart, of whom then shall I be afraid?" I read the twenty-third Psalm reminding me, "Though I walk through the valley of the shadow of death I will fear no evil for He is with me." Though darkness surrounded us, I began to take comfort in knowing it was merely a harmless shadow of death of which God told me not to be afraid.

Tony read the chart at the end of her bed and saw seven major complications listed. Anna had a swollen septum in her heart. She had a liver condition, and any time she cried she turned blue. Anna's blood glucose level at one point was two, a level that should have put her in a coma. Her abdomen was distended due to a blockage in her bowels. She had a heart murmur. She was severely jaundiced and was placed under intense phototherapy. And she had "parental-infant separation". Tony and I also suffered from "parental-infant separation".

After talking to the cardiologist, we realized that God in His mercy helped prepare the medical staff. One month earlier a little boy at the high-risk center had the exact same heart condition that Anna had. Because of this young man, the doctors were able to identify the problem with her septum more quickly and, consequently, knew to prescribe the exact medicine she needed. Time was of the essence. The experienced neonatal team had already had a dress rehearsal before Anna's arrival.

Of the six preemie nurseries, Preemie Six was for the nearly recovered babies who might be going home soon. Slowly Anna made the progression through the preemie units. Somewhere between Anna's stay at Preemie One and Preemie Three, I was in the hotel room late one night with the television tuned to a Christian network. A prayer line with a toll-free number was displayed across the screen. I decided that having more people praying would be a comfort to me personally. When I finally got through to the volunteer counselor on the other end of the line, he asked me a question. "Tell me, is there any hope for your daughter?" I remember standing in front of the mirror feeling disgusted and outraged at his question. "What do you mean is there any hope?" I replied indignantly. "Of course, there is hope. Jesus is our hope." It was that night that I found the verse that became my manna each new day. "I will take refuge in God and not man."

The words in Psalm 42:5 reassured me by asking, "Why so downcast, oh my soul? Put your hope in God." I found myself lovingly embraced by the God of comfort and hope, reminding me to trust Him. We revisited Psalm 118 time and again declaring over Anna, "You will live and not die and declare what God has done forever." Prayer had become our lifeline in this tumultuous storm as we desperately worked to anchor our lives to His Word.

Sometimes, though, my confidence would waver because Anna's hold on life appeared so fragile. For the first time I boldly asked myself, "What if she does die? Will your love for God be the same? Would you ever trust Him again?"

CHAPTER EIGHT
SEEING BEYOND THE REPORT

Each day I struggled to find my balance between the thin lines of surrender and aggressive faith. Death's shadow had not been a stranger to us. Early in our marriage when we were traveling on the road in a full time ministry, I vividly remember calling my parents on a pay phone in Florida to announce that their first grandchild was expected. Only two short weeks later, however, Tony called my parents back from a suburb outside Atlanta, Georgia, informing them that I had lost our first baby. Ironically, the angel of death visited us at a church named the River of Life.

I remembered the short hospital stay in Georgia where a doctor had convinced me that I must have a D&C. During my recovery, my husband temporarily left my side one night to fulfill his preaching commitments at a church. Lying in my bed, I looked out over the inner courtyard as I cried. I felt alone, confused, and uncertain; both Tony and I longed for a family. While I stared into the courtyard through a stream of tears, I saw a small bird. It seemed as if he were looking in each and every window in pursuit of something or someone. Then it flew to my windowsill as if satisfied to find his assignment. As I watched, I realized that the bird was a sparrow. In that moment I heard comforting words deep within my being. "Do not fear; you are of more value than many sparrows." Jesus' words in Matthew 10:31 assured me that I was not alone.

We again witnessed death's face on the first Christmas morning in our marriage when sudden darkness interrupted my eyesight. My loss had been great, and yet I dared not grieve too long for I was determined to enjoy the sight I had left. The damage to my eyes had not diminished my vision for life. I resolved not to let shovels of hopelessness and depression bury me. Little did I know then that I would continue to face death over the next years as my eyes kept changing. I would mourn each loss and struggle to accept the departure.

Now I stood once more to face the potential intruder, death, who threatened to rob me of my firstborn daughter. I sat on the edge of my motel bed, contemplating my choices as I asked, "What if?" My weary mind practiced what I would say and how I would respond.

I knew the passages that assured me that the sacrifice of Jesus at Calvary had made death's sting powerless. Why then did I feel the threat of more pain and disappointment? What could a godly man of long ago have based his resilience on when he boldly declared that even if death came, he would still trust? On what basis could I fight for Anna's life? My mind raced as I gathered data from scriptures I had buried deep in my heart over the years. One thing I knew—this battle could be won only with God's help and intervening hand. I decided not to focus on death but life. Anna was still breathing and that was enough to cause me to hope in a new day. I resolved to trust and not waver. If death came, then I would meet it head on with the grace and ability that my Father would give to me. I was confident that I would not be alone but accompanied by One who had victoriously dominated death's grip. In the meantime, I knew that the battle was intense, and I would need every faith arsenal that I could find in His Word.

My mind and soul were flooded with Psalm 118, verse 17: "You will live and not die and declare what God has done forever."

Proverbs 4:22 reminded me that "The Word of God was life and health to our flesh." I already had an understanding that the literal meaning of health in that verse was medicine. Of course! My strategy became clear from this point forward. As long as Anna was living, there was hope. I would apply the medicine of God's word while the medical profession applied their best treatment.

I would couple every physician's report with God's word, seeing the HOPE in Christ. In the midst of the hopelessness of the situation, I had to choose whom to listen to each day. As I watched the doctors and nurses administer their finest medicine to our sick little girl, I would apply His medicine with every visit. Whether I was standing by Anna's isolette or, on rare occasions, holding her, I would speak the Word of God over her. My constant declaration to Anna became, "You shall live and not die and declare what God has done forever."

The skilled medical team worked meticulously to care for Anna those three long weeks. Tony and I diligently bathed our daughter in passages of scriptures and endless prayers as we held on believing that God could do the impossible. At times, I saw the nurses express amusement while I sang the Word to her and prayed, but I was not deterred.

Each day I would ask the doctors for a report of Anna's condition. Up until the day we carried her home from the hospital, they gave us no hope of her recovery. During the twenty-one day marathon, I pored over the Psalms. I found more scriptures to declare in prayer, comforting words that helped undergird my personal faith. I was grateful to know that in the center of crisis I didn't need to be convinced of God's love. I had already come to know and believe it. I remember some distinct things that changed Anna's course and ours forever. God had been my welcomed Father for many years, and His goodness motivated me to trust Him more. I was familiar with the price that Jesus Christ, God's only Son, had paid for my salvation and peace. I reflected on Psalm 107:20, "He sent His word and healed them and delivered them from all of their destruction." Nahum 1:7 assured me, "The Lord is good, and a stronghold in the day of trouble; and He knows those who trust in Him."

In the middle of quoting scriptures and declaring them in prayer, I was often tempted to wonder, "What if it doesn't work?" Instead, I found that the heart of my Savior was touched by our infirmities. The battle was to trust.

The following day I walked through the now familiar hospital doors with a holy determination to administer medicine of a heavenly nature that the professionals didn't know about. When Anna was moved from the most intensive high-risk unit to the next level, I was permitted to hold her more frequently. Even though the moments of bonding with my daughter were short, I maximized our time together. I would warmly tell our little girl of my love and the Savior's love for her life. I commissioned her to fight the good fight and live. Each day I would quote over her my theme verse for this war zone. I stated it, prayed it, and sang it. "Anna, you will live and not die and declare what God has done forever." The nurses watched my every move and I could see that some continued to snicker at my determination. Every day I would ask the doctors if there was any hope, and they would shrug their shoulders. No wonder God had previously given me the scripture, "I will take refuge in God and not man." Apparently, they had not seen the reports I had seen from the Great Physician. His medicine would make a difference in time.

As our battle for Anna's life continued for three weeks, I related to Daniel in the Old Testament. He, too, found himself in a confrontation that lasted twenty-one days. What intrigued me the most was God's answer to Daniel. He told him that He had heard his prayer on the first day, but it took twenty-one days for the answer to be evident. What if Daniel had quit believing God on day twenty? I also remembered Winston Churchill's powerful directive in a speech to his nation on the eve of World War II, when England was in the battle for its life. His inspiring words were, "Never, never, never give up." I found myself encouraged by the examples of people who held on with tenacity. In the midst of our war, we only could stand one day at a time.

One afternoon, ten days into the battle, three friends called to say they wanted to see me. Though I appreciated their loving concern, I made a decision that I fear hurt them badly. The three, who had delivered babies around the same time Anna had been born, announced they were coming to visit with their newborns. I refused their visit, even though I was afraid they would not understand why. However, I was fully aware of my vulnerability and knew that I could not bear to see the arms of my friends full of new life while my baby was fighting for each breath. When I hung up the phone, I distinctly felt their rejection as I battled with anger over their insensitivity. I wept uncontrollably, realizing that Tony and I had no one but God. We allowed few to visit us because our emotions were fragile and our greatest enemy was unbelief. We tried to protect ourselves and stay focused on the battle at hand as we knew we could not afford any distractions. No one knew how to help us and even I did not know what I needed. I fortified all the foundations of faith as I struggled not to be moved by the ominous medical reports that left little or no hope. I was not confident of the outcome of our explicit trust in the Great Physician, but I knew it was our responsibility to choose life while Anna was still breathing. The results belonged to the God of our salvation.

At one point there was a major change in direction as we prayed for Anna's recovery. One night my fasting husband paced the floor praying for Anna's heart, which we thought was most critical. However, Tony felt an urgent prompting of the Lord to focus on her abdominal area. In addition to listening to this instruction, he called others, and a network of prayer support went to work.

The next morning, following my usual routine, I phoned the hospital to talk to the night nurse before the shifts changed. I always asked, "What is the status of Anna McWilliams and how was her night?" This particular morning I was especially interested in her condition because I knew that a surgeon had been scheduled to do exploratory surgery. The nurse would typically reply, "There has been no change." There was nothing different about this morning's answer, until the nurse suddenly remembered, "Oh, wait one moment. Anna passed a cork of a substance in the night. We're canceling this morning's surgery." "YES," I screamed when I hung up the phone. It was our first ray of sunshine and our hope was rekindled. We became ecstatic over every messy diaper after that. Thank God for a praying husband who was not afraid to heed his Father's instructions.

From that moment Anna grew increasingly stronger. Each major problem began to improve over the ensuing days. The doctors were amazed and yet did not feel confident enough in her improvement to ever give us a hint of hope. A battle was waged between what I could see and the unseen hand of an intervening Great Physician. I struggled with the medical information because it was in conflict with His written reports in the scriptures. I felt a rushing undercurrent constantly tugging at me as we trudged upstream in the river of impossibilities. It was imperative that my arms be linked with my husband's as we firmly held to the hand of our experienced Guide and Protector.

With no notice, the day came when the doctors announced that they were going to release Anna. We could take her home. Her health had stabilized and all threatening conditions had disappeared, except for one. She still had a heart murmur that would have to be monitored for the rest of her life. Astonished by her abrupt release, we quickly began to pack for home. God had answered our cries.

Anna was discharged from the hospital the day before Tony's twenty-fourth birthday. What a gift to be given to a new daddy. On the birthday morning, we sat Anna in her infant carrier on our breakfast counter. Tony and I sat on stools and watched our miracle for hours as she slept in peace. We laughed, cried, and reflected on the awesome mercy of a God who could do the impossible. Tony's birthday was celebrated by new life that had come to bless our home.

We were too excited to fully realize how fatigued we were from the battle we had fought for Anna's life. However, now that she was under my watchful care, I hardly allowed myself to sleep. I kept Anna's bassinet next to our bed and constantly watched to make sure she was breathing. She never left our side. My challenge was to settle my nervous jitters as a new mom and ignore the negative reports that had been planted in my mind. I dreaded the next visit with the cardiologist. I just wanted to be left alone to enjoy the prized gift that we had been given.

Three months after Anna's release, we returned to the hospital for heart tests. The attending heart technician remembered Anna and her physical battle. In the middle of his observation he blurted out, "Oh my! Oh my!" Fearing one more trial, I anxiously thought, "Oh dear, now what?" He kept testing her heart, and listening to every sound in her chest cavity, and then once again he said, with more drama in his voice, "Oh my! This cannot be the same child."

Her heart was normal. The murmur was gone.

CHAPTER NINE
SEEING BEYOND
THE MIRACLE

Music filled the house and bright sunbeams penetrated the living room as I grabbed the handle of the vacuum cleaner. Anna was strapped onto me inside her baby knapsack while we set out to clean the house together. I was rarely without Anna as I hovered over my gift from above, never wanting her out of my sight. God had heard my cry and at last we had been given a child. Our trials and victories were a testimony of His faithfulness and mercy. I wasn't going to let go of her easily.

Tony had accepted a full-time pastor position in a town thirty miles from our home. I remained busy with ministry invitations, speaking and singing at other Christian organizations and churches. I had learned to compensate for the change in my eyesight but still found it frustrating that no glasses would restore my vision. If I wanted to read the Bible, I had to use a large print version along with a magnifier. Tony and I quickly learned how to work together as a team with my limited eyesight, especially in the care of Anna. She never even seemed to know the difference between her caregivers, because she was secure in the love and attention we constantly gave her.

Our lives seemed complete. The joy of being the mother of a miracle daughter overshadowed my faltering eyesight. Even though I had long passed the point of seeing precisely, I maneuvered every way I could to keep my driver's license. I feared losing my independence if I had to give up driving. Self-sufficiency had been part of my makeup since childhood. It took a frightening incident to change my mind.

One afternoon Anna and I were a few minutes from home when I suddenly realized I could not see my turnoff or the lines differentiating the lanes of the highway. In a panic, I inched my way down an empty road, only guessing exactly where the path might be. In that brief moment I had come to face the truth. After I found the road that led to our home, I pulled off to the side of the road by a country ditch and breathed deeply to overcome my anxiety. "Gail! What are you doing?" The very child I had agonized over with faith, tears, and the scriptures was now in jeopardy of living because her mother did not know how to make an honest evaluation of her limitations. I knew that if I kept driving, my little girl's life might be in danger, or she could be without a mother to care for her. The price was too great; my prideful independence had to go.

This decision was more painful than all the previous warfare. I could not bear to think about waiting and depending on others to assist me. Would I ever go anywhere by myself again? This loss was excruciating, and I now felt trapped in a dark prison cell, destined to wait for someone's help and not wanting to accept it.

It is humbling to be vulnerable to others. I wondered if I had any value. I no longer felt like the life-giver, only the energy-drainer. How could I help my husband? How would I competently care for my little girl and her growing needs? I had had unlimited faith for Anna's hopeless situation, but I lacked faith for my own predicament.

Unsuccessfully, I tried to blend my fear with my faith. But I came to understand that faith is a pure seed that could not be crossbred with anything else and remain pure. Faith in God alone and explicit trust intersected with doubt and fear. I must choose my course for the days ahead.

A friend had given me the name of some state organizations that helped the visually impaired. I reluctantly made an afternoon appointment for someone to come to my house and tell me about my options in the midst of my faltering sight. I clearly remember the knock at the exact time of my scheduled appointment. I was shocked to open my door to a totally blind man with a white cane. I was outraged. The last person I wanted to talk to was a person who seemingly had lost the battle. In my smug, abrupt manner, I let the man enter my house, but I was indignant. Who on earth had sent a visual reality of the very thing I feared the most—total blindness? My heart shut down and I stamped "denial" on my case from the outset.

I sat across the room from this courageous man who had great abilities; nevertheless, I was deaf to his challenge and pleas. I wanted nothing to do with any blind person because I was determined to fight off my own "temporary" setback. If I were to listen to his instructions or accept his training, I would only be saying "yes" to defeat, and my battle for hope would be lost. I cried aloud in my head, "Send me someone to help me use what eyesight I have left. Don't make me jump to the end of my journey so suddenly." I sat tempted to make faces at the caseworker to test if he were truly blind. My thoughts were childish as I internally threw a temper tantrum, refusing his help. I wanted God to heal me as he had healed my daughter. Instead, I sat glaring at this man, the embodiment of what I rejected and feared the most.

Depression and hopelessness assaulted me from every side. Could I find the inner strength to once again trust the Great Physician? I had no choice if I were to ever make it out of this landslide of muddied emotions.

I buried myself in more activities than the normal person would because I had something to prove to the world and to myself. Working with the church, speaking wherever I was asked, and lavishing our little girl with attention became my daily focus. I poured over the scriptures to find passages that would help me concentrate on the miraculous. The "rest" of faith was more like the frantic scurrying to just survive. The outside of my life looked strong, but inside I was crumbling with fear. I learned how to displace my fears and think about everything but the possible blindness. My acting skills were prize winning as I fooled everyone into thinking I could still see. It was important to me to hide my flaws. However, the mask I wore held me in more bondage than simply fear of telling the truth. I also feared rejection, wondering if others would treat me as I had treated the blind social worker. I could not even use the word "blind," because I refused to give it credence in my life. Instead, I creatively used terms like "visually challenged" or "impaired eyesight." The word "handicapped" disgusted me, and I scheduled more events and activities to prove I was not weakened or disabled in any way. I resented my situation, and I was determined not to be any different from others.

The long days ahead would quickly turn into years of restlessness and incessant searching. I lacked a mature faith and thorough trust in the One who held my life in His hands. In time, I would learn to admire and respect people with disabilities as victorious conquerors who, along with me, refused to be put on a shelf. Through years of tears, questions, and fears, I began to rest in being honest with others and God about my limitations. His ability counteracted any disability I might face. His vision would replace eyesight with the potential of seeing more than the human eye could dream. His power would offset my challenges, and His courage would dispel my discouragements. His strength was exchanged for my weakness, and my anxieties were absorbed by His peace. His faith would substitute my doubts as I learned to depend on Him alone for every part of my life.

In the course of walking in my newly found revelation, I had to contend with a crowd of conflicting voices. Not all the cheers from the stands were in step with my performance in the race set before me. Some would shout, "If only you had more faith." Others would say, "Your sickness is because of your sin." After being fully interrogated to determine if I was forgiven, then they would suggest, "It must be the sin of your parents or a line of ancestors." My prejudice with the blind state caseworker was mirrored by the prejudice of some church members towards me—my disabilities were repulsive and unacceptable to them.

I would weigh the words of my self-proclaimed counselors as I searched for answers, too. But my vulnerability often kept me open to their insensitivities and unsound advice. No one wanted freedom more than I did from this unwelcome intruder and its consequences.

I have since decided that people mean well but often react to life instead of responding to it. Despite their good intentions, some people say the dumbest things. I am certain that they think they need to find answers to help others, but I think they are looking for answers to help themselves. If they see someone's pain and can justify it, then they are excused from thinking that they, too, might one day have to drink from the cup of suffering. They are not at peace with themselves as they grope for answers to other people's problems. With so much attention on the lives of others, there is little time that has to be spent on their own. In reality, it is when we face the darkest places of our lives that we begin to look for a saving light.

As a young, inexperienced warrior in unexplained suffering, I had to look only to the God of Comfort and Hope to help me. He alone was my answer. God had given me a miracle once; could I trust Him for more?

CHAPTER TEN
SEEING BEYOND THE CHOICE

There was a chill in the air that fall morning as we walked briskly to the doors of the medical center, after finding a place to park in the crowded parking garage. As the crisp, cool air brushed up against my face, I took a deep breath, welcoming the beginning of my favorite season. Across the road was a large park with great mighty oak trees. The leaves were changing and brilliant autumn colors were upon us. Oh, how I wished we were strolling the trails and hills of the park instead of advancing toward the dreaded doctor's appointment. My stomach was unsettled as I wondered what new discoveries he would make today. Transition was again beginning to take place all around us.

It had been nearly three years since my eyesight had first been interrupted. Now, three and a half months pregnant with our second child, my husband and I had returned to this famous Midwest hospital to be evaluated again by eye specialists. Doctors had already diagnosed diabetic retinopathy, and a devastating pattern had begun to unfold. Once again, the effects of pregnancy caused the blood vessels in my eyes to hemorrhage.

We walked down the sterile halls of the hospital clinic, and I took a seat as my husband registered my name with the receptionist. The appointment that day was not simply a visit with a doctor but was instead a full examination, an exhausting four to six hours, part of the yearly research on my eyes.

As a young girl, I had been enrolled in a research program that monitored diabetic children and the effects of this disease on the patients' lives. Of course, I did not appreciate the wonderful value of the research, which meant medical treatment my family could afford. I only knew that I hated every test.

The appointments consisted of frequent dilation of my eyes; this always caused a burning sensation that made me weep and seemed never-ending. My doctors would measure the pressure in my eyes, a complicated and uncomfortable test. I would lie quietly on a table while a metal mechanical arm placed on my eye calculated its every motion. Any movement might affect the test negatively. I remained still, staring at the ceiling. I longed to preoccupy myself but instead was annoyed that there was no music playing and no funny pictures to watch on the ceiling.

The next test required extreme concentration. I placed my face in a large global screen, rested my chin on a stand, and stared at a little hole in the middle of the screen. I waited for any sudden movement from any direction and then responded quickly by tapping the desk when I saw the first sign of light in my peripheral vision. Though it was a simple request, it became maddening because, after a while, my mind would play tricks on me. As I concentrated on detecting the sudden movements of the objects, my head began to hurt. My dilated eyes were blurry and burning, and I wondered if I was passing or failing. How strange that even eye tests become a self-induced competition. When I was a child, I so badly wanted to do well on the tests.

The worst test of all was when I was moved to another office to have pictures taken of my eyes. My job was to keep my eyes open while I rested once again on a chin guard while some unseen person took hundreds of pictures of my eyes. With the intense lights so close to my dilated eyeballs, my first inclination was to back away from the intruding brightness; however, my head was held by the assistant's hand to minimize my natural reaction. My eyes cried from the shock and torment. I often wondered if this process was used during war to torture enemies to bring them to a full breaking point, compelling them to tell all. I was ready to confess anything they wanted to hear just to get the researcher to stop this inhumane procedure. Ironically, I wondered if all the penetrating bright lights flashing in my eyes could make me go blind.

After four to five rolls of film in the canister, I sat back in my chair, relieved to close my eyes and enjoy the darkness. However, even with my eyes closed, I saw the lights, as my eyes and mind adjusted. I walked back with the medical assistant, drained from the tests but knowing more awaited me at the end of the hall. As I took my seat, the nurse announced that she needed to dilate my eyes one more time before the doctor would see me. Finally, I had reached the end of the maze and had earned the right to see another person in a white coat holding an ever-expanding file in his hand. The process was successful in many ways because, by the end of the day, I was weary and vulnerable and had no expectations or fears of any news. I simply knew I was about to the finish line of the long marathon that I had been forced to run.

This time, when the doctor began to speak, he was gravely serious and confident. He made it clear to me that my eyes were changing and that my eyesight was in danger. He said firmly, "Today you will have to choose your baby or your eyes." Without missing a heartbeat, I replied, "The decision is made. I choose my baby."

CHAPTER ELEVEN
SEEING BEYOND THE FEAR

The doctor seemed startled that his words could not bully me into his way of thinking. He stood to his feet and slammed shut my medical file, obviously preparing for a hasty retreat. His parting words delivered a stinging rebuke: "What a foolish decision."

As the door slammed between us, I found myself alone in a cold room with everything out of focus. The room was quiet. It was then that a familiar Voice resonated with comforting power in the depths of my being. It declared, "I have set before you Life and Death; Blessing and Cursing. Choose Life that you and your descendants may live."

The voice was as familiar to me as that of a shepherd speaking reassuringly to one of his flock. The words were from a favorite scripture in Deuteronomy 30:19, buried long ago in the treasure of my soul, as if I had painstakingly committed it to memory for such a time as this.

Strangely emotionless but with an uncommon resilience, I felt my spirit immediately rise. I knew I had spoken the truth. I knew I had made the right decision. The chilling atmosphere of the examining room was held at bay as if by an invisible hand, as these words of life warmed me within. Together, the Great Physician and I stood on the side of Life, having a keen vision for the generations that were yet to come.

I cannot recall the three-hour drive home from the draining examination. I do know that I never questioned my decision. God's grace had given me His ability to make the right choice. Little did I know how many lives would be affected by that sudden decision. I had embarked upon the River of Life, and its power had given me strength and determination for the moment of conflict. Its forceful current would take me to the open waters of trust—in time.

My first concern and intense prayer became that of looking for a new obstetrician to care for me. The old doctor, whom we called the "butcher," had announced his retirement when I returned for my six-week checkup with our first miracle daughter, Anna. He angrily told me that it was patients like me who had convinced him to go into retirement. Then, with his finger in my face, he sternly told me never to think about having any other babies. I was shocked by his angry words, as I affectionately held my new bundle of victory. We had won the battle. Possibly his retirement was driven by the fear of a lawsuit. Months later, a nurse told us in confidence that the hospital worried about this possibility, as well. We, on the other hand, had never considered such a thought because we were too engaged in the battle for life.

Now that we had a traumatic history of seeing that our pregnancies were different from the norm, we diligently worked on finding a knowledgeable Christian doctor to help us navigate through some potentially troubled waters. A physician friend of ours from southern Illinois helped us through this process. He looked through his listings of Christian doctors who were practicing in our state and immediately called to tell us there was one in a city about an hour from our home. The distance was secondary to the desire to have this baby delivered by experienced, skilled hands.

On our first visit to this wonderful, father-like physician, we told him about finding his name in a Christian directory of doctors. He looked puzzled and said he had never been part of any organization like the one we mentioned. In fact, he went on to say, his wife went to church and was the religious one of the family. He did, however, embrace life and its value. While talking to us, he pointed to the picture of his wife and their seven children. We felt comforted that we would not have to justify fighting for the life of our second baby. He agreed to give me his support and care if I also would agree to see an endocrinologist who specialized in diabetic pregnancies. This was the gold mine we needed. The team was now taking shape as we all prepared to win in this game of endurance and skill.

The endocrinologist that had been referred to us made all the difference in the world. He was a knowledgeable English doctor who stayed current with diabetic research. When I first visited his office, I asked why he had chosen to be a specialist in diabetic pregnancies. My heart was moved when he shared that, as a young intern in England, he had witnessed the complications related to diabetic pregnancies, often resulting in death. What he had observed as a young man had influenced his present passion, and I was its beneficiary.

The doctor visits were frequent and the monitoring ever so thorough. The many mistakes and sloppy care that I had been subjected to during the first nearly fatal pregnancy had now become obvious in light of my new medical care. The Great Physician had, indeed, been working overtime to protect us, in spite of it all.

We were on top of our game as we prepared for the final trimester, yet I felt myself slipping into a hole of fear. During Anna's naptime, I would sit in the dark, rocking the expected baby within my womb. As I rocked, I played mental tapes of all of the doctors' concerns, repeating the overwhelming statistics that fed my growing fear. I would cry as I rocked, pleading with God to protect me from one more tragedy. I now knew too much. My vision, along with my eyesight, quickly changed as I looked at the circumstances. I was afraid and alone. Where was my resilience and determination? The battle had become too hard and I could not see anything but fear.

Finally, the months passed in spite of the darkness, and the medical team sought each other's counsel as they developed strategies for my delivery. The sonograms had shown that I was carrying another girl and her name was already picked out: Lindey. The doctors had determined that it would not be safe to carry my second daughter to full term. However, the critical question was, "When should she be taken by cesarean birth?" They decided that I would be put in the hospital one month before Lindey was due to be born.

I survived the days of waiting by wrapping myself in praise music and the Word of God. When I checked into the hospital, I requested a private room so I could control my atmosphere and surroundings. I came loaded with a tape player to play tapes of the Bible and an endless selection of worship music. I had no idea that I would be in my bunker for fifteen long days during this war with fear. My focus was on surviving for two with the daily rations of His strength and hope. To my amazement, I found that there was an endless supply of grace, peace, and faith for me each dawn as I gazed into His face. The Lord undergirded my restlessness with His peace as I paced the halls waiting my day of deliverance. I was reassured that the threatening torment which tried to strike me with the poison of fear was rendered powerless because of Calvary. Jesus had defeated my foe and exchanged my fears with Hope. The doctor's reports took a back seat to the report of the Great Physician.

After I had been in the hospital for eight days, the doctor ordered an amniocentesis that would allow the team to decide if the development of our second daughter was far enough along to assure her safety outside my womb. My doctor warned that if we waited too long, my life could be in danger, as well as our baby's life. I was eager for something to happen; the days had dragged on too long.

Tony came over early to join me for the test. As I was rolled into the small surgery room, a crowd of nurses and doctors encircled my bed. Even though my eyesight had become impaired, I saw the length of the needle the doctor would insert in my womb. At once I turned to look in my husband's face for comfort. I saw his tender eyes of unwavering love for me and felt his nerves of steel.

The goal was to retrieve the exact amount of fluid without hurting the child that innocently lay within. A team member gave me a local anesthetic, and the doctor stuck the long, piercing needle in my belly. The sudden violation made Lindey roll quickly to one side of my womb, far away from the sharp, uninvited intruder. Instead of clear liquid, the syringe was filled with a mixture of blood. After a second try, the doctor probed into areas that were not numbed. With each attempt the room filled with more tension. My original obstetrician had removed himself from my case due to his own personal crisis, and now I was in the hands of a substitute. It became obvious that his name was probably not listed in the directory of Christian physicians because the pressure had led him to be profane as he continued to probe unsuccessfully. I, on the other hand, had been given courage in the midst of the uncomfortable trial. With each new stab I would look deeper into my husband's eyes as though to ask, "How much more?" We grasped each other's hands so tightly that the circulation was affected. Finally, after the ninth try, the doctor said we would have to do it again in a few days. The dam broke as warm tears fell uncontrollably down my cheeks. We all surrendered to defeat.

Three more days passed with my name on the schedule for one more amniocentesis. Oh, how I dreaded the thought of doing that one more time. Early on March 30th, before breakfast could be served, my endocrinologist arrived. Though my team of doctors worked closely together, everyone was listening carefully to my endocrinologist as his expertise in diabetic pregnancies helped provide significant guidance at this crucial time. I vividly remember that he paced back and forth at the foot of my bed, thinking aloud. As he weighed all the possible risks of waiting against the dangers of taking the baby by cesarean section too early, I thought of the movie, "Fiddler on the Roof". The scene was of Tevya talking aloud to an unseen personality in the heavens, halted between two opinions, while all of life stood frozen in time.

As I watched my perplexed doctor seek the answers he needed, my hope was that his counsel would come from the Great Physician who had never left my side. The doctor finally turned to me with his decision. He said we would take the baby in two days on April 1st. "I have not waited all this time to have a baby on April Fool's Day," I replied. He laughed, thinking I was joking, until he saw my countenance. "You cannot be serious." "Oh, yes, I am very serious. You can take her any day before or after, but I will not give birth on April Fool's Day." Amazed, the doctor stood at the end of my bed studying my face. "Okay. Then we will wait a few more days and you will have the amniocentesis test once more." I agreed to our negotiations as he ordered the attendant to serve my breakfast.

It was just minutes after I had finished breakfast that my doctor returned, saying, "I've changed my mind. We'll take the baby today." I had only two pressing questions—"Would my husband be able to drive the distance on such short notice to be with me for the birth?" and "What will happen to the breakfast that I just ate before surgery?"

Within a short amount of time I was prepped for surgery and the enema had been successful. Surely my breakfast had not had time to inflict me with even one calorie. My hurried husband made the hour trip in record time to join the team for the delivery of our second daughter. Tony left my side to scrub up for his front row seat at the birth of his daughter. In order to prove he could stay with me, he had to show the doctors that he could focus on a sponge filled with blood. He passed the test and, like a pro, settled down on a stool near my head, even though the residing doctor had invited him to be at the grand opening. I, on the other hand, lay once again on the cold table with my arms intertwined with tubes, surrounded by monitors and wearing an oxygen mask to help me breathe. The room was filled with professionals who had been trained for this moment. We all awaited the outcome as the doctor pulled the small bundle from my womb.

What a difference this birth had been from that of the butcher's knife. I heard my little girl cry as the room sighed with relief. A nurse inquired, "What's her name?" and I gratefully stated, "Lindey."

In the time it took to sew me back together, my little girl had finished her first tests, and the scores were posted. She was quickly bundled in a warm blanket and taken to the high-risk unit for observation. I might have been saddened not to hold my newborn, but I faced a new challenge, one that no one had expected. I went into shock. I felt out of control as my body shook violently, and the nurses piled more and more warm blankets on me.

Tony had followed Lindey down to the high-risk unit to hear firsthand if she was healthy. From where I lay, he seemed to be gone for days. Through chattering teeth, I asked someone to tell me, "Is my baby still alive?"

CHAPTER TWELVE
SEEING BEYOND SHOCK

As I lay in the recovery room shaking uncontrollably with my body in shock, a kind and gentle hand touched my trembling shoulder. "Gail, she's beautiful," I heard my husband whisper. Once again, I had been denied holding my newborn, but Tony had been able to embrace his second daughter before she was whisked away to the isolette in the high-risk preemie unit. Her condition was uncertain.

Tony showed me a Polaroid picture of our little six-pound, one-ounce girl, Lindey Christene, and told me her hair was thick and black and her features petite. Tony gently warned me that they were checking Lindey's lungs and that her condition could be serious. Thankfully, she did not have all the critical problems that her sister, Anna, had at birth. The expert team of caring doctors had made a world of difference.

Within hours, my shock subsided. Lindey's medical difficulties were diminishing as we heard more updates on her condition. The doctors who had remembered Lindey's older sister, Anna, now three and a half years old, remarked at the differences they saw in this little McWilliams girl. In spite of the fact that her lungs weren't fully developed, the threat of any lung disease was gone. She was treasured like a Lindey Star Sapphire lying under the lights as we waited for her bilirubin to be lowered in phototherapy. Lindey's father kept busy traveling from one floor to another as he checked on both of his hospitalized ladies. The nurses remarked with astonishment how determined both women were to get on with life.

The thrill of my heart was to be wheeled down to see my youngest daughter for our first visit. I was surprised when a nurse unplugged her lights for a short time and placed Lindey in my arms. Overcome with an inexpressible joy, I cradled the gift God had given me. The pain of my incision was totally numbed by the satisfaction of holding the trophy at the end of an incredibly long race. I had been crowned in the winner's circle, and I heard the applause of heaven. Cradled in my arms was the child that the eye doctors called a foolish decision. One more time they were wrong. How ironic that she was almost born on April Fool's Day. Contrary to their advice, the God of Wisdom had protected this new little lamb from the slaughter of man's best-laid plans. What was the destiny that awaited this new life that had fought so hard to get here?

I was ecstatic over the news that Lindey and I were both being released after one week of healing and were going home together. At last, I had arrived at semi-normal motherhood. I later laughed when I told people that Lindey had to be kept in the warmer for one extra week because she was not fully done. No day seemed more perfect than when we both were released to leave the hospital together. God had kept us safe in the midst of the storm. No one had been lost.

Our house was a center of activity. The joy of new life distracted me from the fact that the pregnancy had caused further deterioration of my eyesight. I rejoiced to be the mother of two little girls. Our challenges were constant, yet never insurmountable. My little girls didn't even notice that I had lost so much of my eyesight. They loved me because I was their mommy. Life was full and exciting.

However, with our growing family and mounting children's paraphernalia, we began to search for a larger house near the church where Tony was now pastoring. God surprised us with a house of our dreams. Its spaciousness and gracious setting was God's bonus. I always thought it came as a gift to our children. I wondered what we would put in all the empty spaces of our new house.

I soon had my answer. One morning I awakened my husband to help me see something. He had become very used to this pattern, a constant interruption of his time. It was just after dawn, and he grumbled a bit to have to see for me even before his own eyes had time to adjust to a new day. I led him into the bathroom and asked him to read the results of a test I had taken. Stunned, he said, "Gail, you're pregnant!"

I no longer had to wonder what would fill our big house for it was obvious—more children. My only concern was telling my family our news. Most rejoice at the announcement of a new arrival, but not my family. They loved children, but they also knew how very dangerous another pregnancy could be for the baby and also for me. My heart was torn because I knew that there could be no greater news than to see our family increased. Our wealth was growing.

One Saturday afternoon during a visit by parents and siblings, we all were sitting in the family room conversing normally. I glanced in my husband's direction with a look that said, "You tell them!" I stood and forced a small cough to announce, "Do it now because I'm leaving!" I knew that Tony would need some kind of transition into this unexpected news, so I asked, "Is Colonel Dobbie coming for a visit soon?" This man was a godly, family friend who lived in Israel. His visits always coincided with my pregnancies, and he was a very special prayer intercessor for us. I thought mentioning his name would be a good segue for Tony's announcement and prepare my family in a subliminal way. I then left the room to tend to a buzzing dryer in our second floor laundry room. I remember looking out the window as I changed loads, praying that God would once again carry my family along on this bumpy road. I despised feeling guilty that I desired children, because it cost so very much in every way. Slowly, I adjusted the washer and dryer to give Tony more time to make the announcement. Within minutes, I came bouncing down the stairs and into the family room. I was dismayed to see the room gravely quiet with family members crying. For a brief moment I wondered just what news Tony had delivered to the distressed audience. Their mourning made me think I should have worn black that day. "Hey guys, the battle is hard enough without having to carry all of you."

Unlike the previous pregnancies, this one progressed quickly. I could find no time to rock and cry or worry over the unknown—life was extremely busy.

As we prepared for the birth of our third daughter, we worked with the same team of doctors, this time with confidence, because they had run this course before. My handpicked obstetrician was back in the practice of delivering babies, and we wanted to let him in on a miracle birth, as he had missed the last one. I remember sitting in his office as we considered when to take this child by cesarean. Once again, the time had to be exact, and our goal was somewhere near week thirty-seven of the gestation. Both the doctor and I had our calendars out, looking at available dates as if we were planning a shopping trip or weekend getaway. My doctor suggested a date in the first part of December. I made my request. "Let's wait until the eleventh of December, because it will be my mother's fiftieth birthday, and I don't have a gift for her yet." He agreed to my mother's birthday surprise and complimented me on my thoughtful selection for a gift.

Giving birth to Holly was a complete joy and my own personal spiritual high. The pregnancy had been perfect, and my eyes had not worsened. It was two weeks before Christmas. The world was decorating their houses and putting up lights to celebrate another miracle birth that had impacted the world. Everyone seemed focused on gifts, and I knew that the gift within my womb would also be celebrated in just a few short days. I had already wrapped two baby dolls and placed them under our Christmas tree so that all of the McWilliams ladies could have a baby in their arms on Christmas morning.

I checked into the hospital before sunrise on the day before my newest daughter's birthday. I was scheduled to have another amniocentesis, which I was dreading. The memory of the last one was still vivid. Much to my surprise, the test was without incident and I felt no pain. The test was successful the first time, and the results indicated that our little girl was ready. I was confident that I had just enjoyed my first Christmas gift, with more to come.

As I waited the night before my baby's deliverance, I experienced His beautiful peace. My room was softly lit as worship music played. All of my visitors had left, and I stood alone, gazing out the hospital window from the eleventh floor. As I looked over the lights of the city with the snow falling, I marveled to think how Mary awaited her own deliverance. She carried the Prince of Peace in whom I now found comfort. I sang softly, "The hopes and fears of all the years are met in Thee tonight." I questioned how her newborn Child of Promise could have been wrapped in swaddling clothes, which were burial clothes of their day. Surely this had pricked her heart as to her Son's destiny. I knew well that my new daughter would never be called on to be the innocent Lamb who would willingly be sacrificed to reconcile the world back to the Father God. His Son had completed that deed in full already. Yet, I wondered what sacrifices she would be required to give with her life. I laid my hands on my expanded belly as I asked the Lord to hold my little one.

My heart was full as I thought about the gift I had found in knowing the Savior personally and the riches He had given to me. In those quiet moments, I smiled to think that I was a Protestant standing in a Catholic hospital, mindful of Mary's willingness to be used by the Lord. I reflected on her answer when the angel first came to tell her of the divine assignment she was being given. Her reply gave me conviction: "Be it unto me, according to your word." Unquestionably, she had lived a life with that declaration perpetually on her lips. Her heart was open to God's request, realizing the great privilege being given her. She had modeled for me in that one statement the desire of my life. I imagined how she must have pondered all of these things in her heart, and I somehow understood in that moment of quietness.

I stepped over to my bed, using the gleam of city lights through my window as a nightlight. As I positioned myself in bed, knowing that the morning would bring a new little voice into my life, I could not help but cry softly as I thought about the love of God and His sending His own Son. He had covered us from the dirt of sin just as the fresh falling snow was blanketing the world just outside my window. I began to praise Him aloud for His mercy and kindness. In the stillness of knowing His love for me, I heard His voice gently say to my heart, "Gail, I would have gone to the cross even if it had been only for you." My tears fell as I felt Him standing near my side, assuring me that I had been born into His kingdom for His purposes ever since I said "yes" to Him as my Savior and Lord from my childhood. The Prince of Peace had come and tucked me into bed, giving me hope for a new day.

Early the next morning Tony and I prepared to meet our newest daughter. The medical team had gathered in my room, in a familiar routine, along with some medical students to assist in our daughter's debut. In this moment, all efforts at modesty were abandoned. My only cry was, "Get this baby out of me so I can breathe again." While I lay on the table, feeling like a beached whale about to be harpooned, I heard a startling statement. A male student nurse blurted out, "Hey, I know who you are. Aren't you Gail McWilliams, the Christian singer I've seen on television?" Mortified, I laughingly gulped air under the oxygen mask and confirmed his discovery. I still wonder how at that moment, under those vulnerable conditions, he had recognized me. What could he have seen?

The birthing process went as fast as the pregnancy, with no complications. Within moments, our daughter was born with strong lungs foretelling her future musical gift. Holly had safely arrived for Christmas and on my mother's birthday.

Unfortunately, my endocrinologist missed my delivery because he was on his way to the airport with plans to fly to Great Britain on holiday. However, he called the hospital from the airport to check our status. He first called the high-risk nursery. When they said there was no McWilliams baby, he quickly stated, "There must be some mistake." He anxiously asked them to transfer him to the intermediate high-risk nursery, but his search was in vain there, too. The doctor now was alarmed because he wondered what could have happened. Holly was missing.

CHAPTER THIRTEEN
SEEING BEYOND
SISTERHOOD

Still searching for the new McWilliams baby, the puzzled, yet determined physician calling from the airport now asked to be connected to the normal hospital nursery. My diabetic specialist who had faithfully walked every step of the way with me during my high-risk pregnancies with Lindey and Holly wanted to make a final check before boarding his plane for Great Britain. This conscientious physician was eager to see the results of his meticulous work. To his amazement, he found our first healthy, newly born daughter in the most unlikely spot: the normal nursery. It was apparent that an awesome team had delivered Holly under the caring eye of the Great Physician.

The nurses placed Holly near the viewing glass. I could not help but painfully remember how the shades were pulled when Anna courageously labored for breath five years earlier. God had been merciful to sustain us. What a contrast these births had been. Holly's thick, dark hair was adorned with a bow the nurses had provided. Her doctors were astonished to see Holly's strength when she raised her head, turning it on the first day and then readjusted herself in her crib. I think we innocently overlooked the warning that perhaps one more strong-willed woman was placed on earth. A third daughter now completed our sorority.

During each of my hospital stays, I had listened to music from home. The praise and worship songs helped me focus on the Master Conductor who was orchestrating my life. One day after Holly's birth, an elderly nun came into my room to replenish the water in my pitcher. Her pace was unusually slow as she diligently carried out her duties. I smiled when she surprised me by twirling around in a bit of a dance, announcing, "I love to worship God, don't you?" She had been enjoying my music while she worked. We began to talk about the faithfulness of God as if we had been long time friends. With excitement, she asked if she could bring another sister to meet me. Within the hour another nun arrived with her guitar. For hours we sat and sang as if we were around a campfire under a starlit sky. Our common ground was in praising the Savior.

Another visiting nun, Sister Jane Marie, had been a friend of my parents for years. They first met during a renewal movement, where Protestants and Catholics met for prayer. When she visited me in the hospital, she placed a stem of holly leaves and berries in my hand, informing me that they told the story of the gospel. The leaves are shaped like a crown, representing the one that had been forced cruelly on Jesus' head before He went to the cross. The white outline trimming the leaf, she explained, represented His purity that cleanses us white as snow. The green spoke of new life in the resurrected Christ. The red berries symbolized the blood of Jesus who took away our sins through His sacrificial love. The leaf can only be sustained by being attached securely to the vine that represents Jesus Christ, the true and living vine.

Sister Jane Marie's gift marked a guidepost for our daughter. My heart was full of awe and gratefulness. The Christmas season had taken on new meaning with such a simple, but extravagant gift.

Surprisingly, in three short days both Holly and I were released. "So, this is what it feels like to be a normal mommy!" I believed that this would be my final stay in a maternity ward. Months before Holly's birth we had taken permanent surgical measures to never have children again. Our season of birthing babies was over. The doctors had convinced us to stop while I still had my remaining sight, and my energies now were needed to raise these little girls.

On the long drive home, I pondered how much my hospital encounter had seemed like a spiritual retreat. When we pulled into our driveway, we saw a decorated Christmas tree and two little girls standing in the tall bay windows with their noses pressed to the glass. They were waiting for more than just Santa's reindeer—they knew their new sister was coming. After hugs and kisses, I walked over and put Holly under the Christmas tree with the bow still on her head. Finally, all of the treasured gifts were arranged under the tree.

There was a feeling of deep contentment as the lights of the holidays began to illuminate the night. The smell of the fire in our fireplace, along with that of the roast being taken out of the oven, had a therapeutic effect. My mother had fixed a special dinner to celebrate the occasion. We had won, and the victory was sweet. Our growing sorority quickly knighted their daddy as the protector of the castle. Psalms had given us clear direction of our mission by stating, "May your daughters be sculpted in palace style." During the dinner prayer, with Holly placed in her infant seat close by, I understood a phrase my father had said: "that which costs much is appreciated most." We were wealthy beyond words.

Our busy household seemed to adapt quickly to one more little girl. I felt great, and my eyes had not changed. God had graced me with the ability to move about with diminished eyesight. For the most part, no one could detect my struggle unless he studied me closely. I never stayed long enough for anyone to detect my limited vision. I also refrained from ever using the word "blind." My days were consumed with an increased drive to take on new challenges, secretly proving to myself that I did not have to be different. Tony calmly absorbed the tremendous challenges and trials we faced due to my dimming vision and our Anna helped too.

I know that firstborns are usually the most responsible children in a family, and this was definitely true with Anna, then only five years old. No wonder the scriptures call the firstborn your "chief strength." Lindey, now twenty months old, was the challenge. She alone wanted to be the caregiver of her baby sister. Lindey needed a watchful eye, and the natural bodyguard of the palace became Anna. She looked over her brood like a mother hen and reported any problems to me. Our girls—their laughter, tears, curls, and lace—filled our house. Tony helped with tasks that required better vision than mine. In addition, he was preparing for his own delivery.

For three years he had been pastoring a small congregation in our city. He had dreamed of starting a new Christian work on the west side of town where there were few churches at the time. His goal was coming to fruition and I stood by to help be the midwife of this church he was building. The anticipation of new church life was invigorating.

Three weeks after Holly was born, we opened our home to a group of Christian believers who met for prayer and Bible study. Each week the group increased in size, and together we asked the Lord to provide a church home for this growing family of faith. The name of the church captured the theme of our family's journey. It was called "Tree of Life." At last, nine weeks after the birth of our third daughter, we arranged to publicly launch the church in a school building. We negotiated a contract that allowed us to rent the school facilities for our Sunday celebration services. Once again, it took a winning team to successfully give birth.

Each week a group of workers would come hours early to move the school cafeteria furnishings and replace them with chairs, sound equipment, flowers, and a pulpit. We had secured two schoolrooms for the Sunday school class and the nursery. No one minded the extra effort to have a Sunday morning place of worship. Everyone was excited about our first service on February 24th. That date remains forever in my memory, because during the long awaited birth, death came to visit again.

On the very day our Tree of Life Church began, the blood vessels in the back of my eyes ruptured without any warning. A slivering, unwanted intruder had surreptitiously slithered into our garden of paradise. The hemorrhaging vessels threatened what precious eyesight remained. Coiled into my thoughts was the taunting question, "Has life cost too much this time?"

CHAPTER FOURTEEN
SEEING BEYOND THE BATTLE

My eyesight was drastically affected, and I was devastated and angry. The timing was more than a coincidence in my mind. I was weary of this persistent enemy who dogged our heels relentlessly. My anger was diminished by the weariness I felt from the past few months of adjustments. I was frantic inside, wondering how I would cope with life. Where was God?

My emotions attacked my faith. I panicked that I would not be able to help my family. I felt ashamed to represent a living God who could do the impossible, and here I was, losing ground every day. How could He use me? I was afraid of the future. How long would it be until I could see nothing? I felt outraged to think we were open targets for the enemy to attack because my resistance was weak. My most vulnerable thought was being angry with God. I resented being dependent on others. How could He betray me and let something bad like this happen to me? It seemed senseless.

I could not discern if this was just postpartum blues or full-blown depression. My deepest concern was that too many were depending on me. I could not fall apart. Each day was busy with our three miracle girls seated around our table. The church was thriving, and the potential was unlimited. In addition, Tony and I hosted a weekly television show that had been broadcast for seven years. I sang often at conventions, and both of us spoke and ministered at Christian meetings during any free time away.

These activities were interrupted as we routinely traveled back to the doctors for checkups, eye evaluations, and pediatrician visits. My doctors expressed their genuine sadness over my loss of more eyesight. This time the loss was more devastating because it appeared that I had totally lost the vision in my right eye. A retina specialist near our home roughly explained, "Your eyes are fried." He then invited Tony to look at the x-rays of my eyes as he explained: "Gail's eyes are like a road map that is splintered, disconnected, and disjointed from any main life-road." I sat across the room, fighting for hope. How strange to refer to my eyes as a crazy map leading nowhere and a breakfast order of "fried" eggs. I wondered exactly what medical school had instructed him. His next statement halted my daydreaming imagination as he sternly said, "She is beyond any help."

I responded defiantly to the doctor's diagnosis. Armed with resilience, I determined that, with the help of the Lord, I would survive and not miss one bit of life. By necessity, I had to be resolute and guard myself from the doctors' discouraging reports, negative circumstances, well-meaning but ignorant Christians, and my own fears. The latter continued to be my most pressing issue. I found myself taking on more projects each passing day with little time to reflect on anything but living.

My diabetic specialist asked if I wanted to participate in a research program for managing weight loss and diabetes. I willingly signed up. My regimen was strict, and the first three months I consumed liquid only. I walked between five and eight miles a day with daily intake of five hundred calories. Obviously, anyone can lose weight starving. I did enjoy being thin for the first time in several years, and that aided my busy life. However, my diabetic condition was unchanged, and I developed a thyroid problem while I was on the program. On my early morning walks, I always took my Walkman and listened to the scriptures. I was in the battle of my life, and I needed support. My growing daughters would watch from the window as I made laps around our neighborhood court while their father babysat. Walking by myself was possible because I could use the eyesight I had left to locate a path marked by the inner curb of our street as it circled around the block. As soon as I came back into the house, Tony would leave for work at the church. We both had fallen into the pattern of helping others because we could not find the answers we needed for ourselves. We humorously declared that our lives would make a survival-of-the-fittest course.

Our burning desire was to help other families be strong. As an outgrowth of that desire, we started a Christian school a year after the church was founded. Our vision was for children to be able to grow and develop in academics and character in a loving, Christian environment. Tony had done his homework thoroughly and we were about to open the school. We were just weeks away from finalizing all the paper work, mission statements, new bylaws, and handbooks.

Our excitement was dramatically interrupted when Tony injured his right wrist in a bizarre accident. Glass that shielded a recessed light in the ceiling shattered, covering Tony with shards as it fell. One sharp sliver of glass pierced an artery in his wrist. As we stood in our family room, Tony began to bleed to death. I could do nothing but scream and jump hysterically. With my diminished eyesight, I couldn't help my husband nor drive him to the hospital. Thankfully, Tony, with great presence of mind acted quickly and placed his thumb in the gaping cut and manually suppressed the bleeding. He created a temporary tourniquet until we could find someone to drive him to the hospital.

Our church building was only minutes away from our house, and my mother volunteered her time there as the secretary/accountant. I called her to come as fast as she could because we had only moments to spare. God must have taken my husband and mother on angel's wings to the hospital that afternoon. I remained behind until someone could watch our children and transport me to the hospital. In the meantime, Anna had gathered the kids from the neighborhood to stand in line to look at the bloody trail throughout the house and on the doors. Tony's cut had produced a fountain of spurting blood that went everywhere, including all over our new white Berber carpeting.

After the rush trip to the hospital, Tony was placed on a gurney and met at the door by the emergency room doctor. When the doctor removed the blood-soaked towel from his sliced wrist, he asked Tony two questions. "Do you have AIDS?" Tony answered, "No." Then he asked, "Did you purposely try to kill yourself?" Tony replied, "No. I'm a pastor." Unmoved, the doctor stared at Tony and asked again, "Like I said, did you want to kill yourself?" Later, I wondered how many distraught pastors he had tended in his career that caused him to persist in his questioning.

The waiting room gradually filled with church members while we waited for any news about Tony in surgery. He had cut a large artery and tendon that demanded some tidy needlework from the surgeon's hand. After a short, two-day stay in the hospital, Tony was released with a cast on his right hand and arm. Now, our home was occupied by the blind and maimed; at least no one was mute. In fact, we were under pressure to finish the final touches of all the training manuals if we were going to keep our schedule for starting the new school. Determined, Tony and I sat down at our dining room table and went to work. Tony would dictate the manual to me, and I would write it out in long hand. Then I would pass it over for him to read aloud. In spite of the pain, we laughed to see our predicament. Anyone else would have given up, we were sure. Our hard work paid off, though, and we met our deadline. Once again, we had experienced a traumatic birth—Tree of Life School. This time Tony was the one on pain pills.

With the start of the new school and the busyness of the growing church, I started going to the office each day to help. God had given me a friend in the church who generously drove me to the store and on any errands. She was a great assistant, and I loved the fact that she laughed at my humorous ways. Our journey together did not seem cumbersome but, instead, fun. Another friend from the church cleaned my house. I still did the majority of the cooking, and my three little helpers assisted me. The girls needed more supervision, so we hired a nanny. One day when I returned from the church, Anna was sitting on the porch, waiting for her parents to come home. After hugging her, I walked into the house and Lindey ran past me yelling, "Mommy's home!" Holly screamed her welcome as she hung on the back of the nanny as though she were strangling her—fully the boss. Our home was out of control. Where were the parents who were responsible for this miracle family? I had been running from what I perceived to be my inability to successfully take care of the greatest treasures in my life. My husband and I had become career-driven ministers, helping save and counsel every other family in our community while ignoring our own. We both had been blind.

Our lives did not change immediately because we had many commitments. The pressure of having others depend on us left us wondering how we would make the needed changes. However, a seed had been planted in our hearts to reverse the direction we were going in order to find a solution for the success of our own family.

God not only was turning our hearts toward home, but He was also opening our eyes to the valuable potential He had placed in our care.

One night after dinner, I had an epiphany. I was finishing the dinner dishes when I suddenly threw down the towel and said aloud, "I am not dead yet." I realized that I had subconsciously been distancing myself from my children. I had used others to help them grow to be independent of me because I thought it would help them survive when I was gone. I had appeared to ignore the doctors' reports, but subconsciously they had affected the core of my being. I desperately wanted to live, yet I wondered if this disease would be all-consuming and prove the doctors right. I had easily chosen life for others, but now I had to choose life for myself. I wondered if I could regain the hearts of my children and be their primary caregiver once again.

My resilience was like a fine, expensive, woven cloth that became more frayed and faded with each new setback. Without warning, my eyes would get worse. Stress seemed to increase their deterioration. I could still see some things, depending on the light, but for the most part everything was blurry. One day I experienced another setback in my visual acuity, and I could not mask my depression any longer. I sat in a dark room numb to everything around me. Each change was another death, and I felt as if I were at a funeral that never ended. With each loss I had to learn to compensate all over again just to function like a normal person. I hated self-pity and tried to resist its companionship. One night my husband held me in his arms after I had inadvertently awakened him. I was in a deep sleep, and he said I began to sob uncontrollably, though I did not know it.

The following morning, Tony took our children with him to the church where they were all enrolled in our nursery and elementary school. After they left, I locked myself in the bedroom and buried my head in the carpet. For hours, I wept and prayed. My emotions changed as often as my eyes. I related to Jacob and the time he had wrestled with God. My match had just started, and I was in the ring with an unseen presence. Long after my words ran out, I asked the Holy Spirit to pray through me according to His perfect will. Ironically, my greatest fears were His guaranteed promises. I feared weakness, and He reminded me that in my weakness He is made strong. I feared fear, to which He responded that His love casts out all fear. Psalm 27 reminded me that "The Lord is my light and my salvation; whom shall I fear? The Lord is the strength of my life; of whom then shall I be afraid?"

On and on my mind was flooded with His Word as I sobbed with my head buried in the carpet, lying face down and lifeless. After crying for hours, I had no more tears. In quietness, I waited. Then I slowly rose to my feet, and as I stood in the middle of the large and spacious room, said aloud, "Thank you for the darkness, for it has made the light so sweet."

WHAT? Is this what the Holy Spirit had been praying through me? I felt anger and betrayal.

CHAPTER FIFTEEN
SEEING BEYOND RELIGION

Troubled, I sat on the edge of my bed. After all these years of walking with the Lord Jesus Christ, I concluded that I really did not know my heavenly Father. Because of my painfully honest assessment, I decided to go back to the Bible and discover for myself the true identity of God. Religion had carved out an image of God that it was comfortable with, but I wanted more.

Ever since I was a child, I desired to walk with the Lord. I remember long talks with my grandmothers about the love of God and about serving Him. My parents were authentic Christians who patterned their lives after the message of Christ. They modeled a lifestyle of Christianity that was not merely attending a church service once a week, when there was nothing better planned. Their commitment to Christ paved the way for me to walk down a solid path where I came face to face with the Savior. However, for years, I had understood that I must discern Truth from religious rules. There was a vast difference between personally knowing the Lord and knowing about Him. Many of His followers are content with man-made rules because it brings some kind of false security; they don't realize that faith and grace are gifts. The work at Calvary's cross and the sacrifice of Christ were complete apart from me. I wish this had been fully revealed to me in the early years of being a pastor's wife. As I was slowly losing my eyesight, it was humbling to be on display for others to monitor my pain and adjustments to this new life's walk. If only I had known more clearly who I was in Christ, then so many hurtful statements by unknowing Christians would not have injured me.

I felt enormous pressure to handle myself in a way that would not cause anyone else to stumble or resent God. If I cried, it was in secret, for the most part. If I questioned the "why of it all," I would do that with only a few trusted believers, behind closed doors. I wanted to protect everyone else's faith while I struggled privately with my own. I was confident of my walk in Christ but perplexed about why I could not appropriate the benefits of Calvary. I lacked confidence in my unquestioning trust in a God who was requiring my full surrender. Unfortunately, my vulnerable state of mind made me a target for other people's comments and judgments.

I often heard that I was not healed because I did not possess enough faith. Consequently, the "rest" of faith, which is discussed in the book of Hebrews, became a place where I worked frantically to measure up. Some comments were purely stupid. A man approached me once at church and said that God had told him, "If I would just be a good wife, then God would heal you." Of course, the implication is that I was a terrible wife. Another suggested that, "If I would stop singing, then I would be healed." This comment confused me. I had sung for the Lord since I was a teen, and now the very gift I had been given from Him stood in the way of His touching me physically? How schizophrenic is that kind of a Father? Nonsense!

One Sunday morning the wife of one of the church leaders cornered me. I stood appalled by the reasoning of her proclamation as she authoritatively said, "Gail, God knew you could not handle your gifts and perfect eyesight, so He had to take one of them." It was senseless to challenge this woman, unless I wanted to hear her glib, over-spiritualized gibberish. I remember thinking, "Why on earth then can you be trusted with eyesight?" As ridiculous as her statements were, they planted seeds of doubt.

I could not discern if I was angry with such people or with myself for just standing there and not challenging their absurd man-made religious judgments. They hid behind a "God-mask" that gave them freedom to say cruel things. Due to my openness to God, I was easily manipulated by the words, "God told me to tell you." In reality, I think the "God-mask" conveniently justified their criticisms of others, while in actuality they were fearful their own inadequacies might be exposed. What I needed most was their encouragement and prayers. I began to think that perhaps I went to church only because my husband was the pastor, and, if this were true, even that reason was becoming less motivating. More and more our ride home from church found me crying. Tony was upset over my lack of protection in church, a place that should have been a refuge, inspiring hope. It would take me all week to find the desire to attend church the next Sunday morning.

Over the years, my family came under scrutiny because of my lack of healing. For the most part, people who wanted the best for us tried to find an answer to our dilemma. Some would inquire, like the stories in the Bible of long ago, "Is it your sin that has caused this to happen?" I regretted not carrying the records of my family tree, because we were often interrogated about the sins of our forefathers. At times, I felt as if I were the guinea pig for exorcism and healing prayer lines. I have been spat on, pushed down, slapped, shaken, and rebuked. The worst part was feeling the pressure to be healed so that another person's faith wasn't shaken. No one wanted an answer to my situation more than I did. I fought anger, confusion, and, most of all, disappointment.

Guilt became a close companion. I vacillated between others' disapproval and God's disapproval. Some of the church zealots wanted results to their spiritual formulas. The medical world wanted me to follow their advice and forego children. I could please no one. I felt alone with nowhere to go. Now, as I sat in the quietness of my bedroom in search of answers, I longed to start all over and begin to know the love of my Father.

Our family vacationed at a beautiful Christian resort in the Carolinas. Before going, we had worked very hard in a variety of ministry projects, and we were almost too tired to even begin the trip. We pressed on knowing that, once we got there, it would be delightful. The trip was uneventful until we pulled through the security gate of this massive complex. Upon crossing the entrance, the blood vessels snapped behind my "good eye," the eye that I depended on to see what little I could still see. I immediately felt the result of the blood in the back of my eyes, because my eyesight was radically impaired. It would be several days later, after the blood drained, before I would know exactly how much damage had occurred. A heavy cloak of despair and hopelessness fell on my soul. Why now?

When we stopped, I opened my door and walked away from the van. Tony asked where I was going. I did not know nor did I care! For the first time, I wanted to walk alone into the woods and simply disappear. I hoped no one would ever find me. I persuaded Tony to let me go alone to find my way to the prayer chapel while he unpacked the van and the children. Deep within my heart, I did not care if I were ever found, because I felt eternally lost already.

Miraculously, I found the building nestled in the beautiful woods. The chapel was moderate in size with center pews where one could sit and reflect. Behind closed doors were small prayer rooms where people could cry out to God in privacy. I requested a room and locked myself in it. A small bench hugged one side of the wall. I turned off the light, lay on the floor under the bench, and began to wail in grief and anguish. My resilience was gone and my faith was wavering. My prayers felt blocked by an impenetrable steel heaven that seemed to bear down on me. My disappointment was irreconcilable, and my dreams had become a nightmare. I could not pray, only cry.

I lost track of time while Tony had lost track of me. He knew, though, that I did not want to be found. I only regained my composure because I could find no more tears. Hesitantly, I opened the door of my prayer closet and stood in the doorway, numb and directionless. Unsure of where to go, I stumbled to a center pew and sat, staring at the cross hanging in the front.

As I sat wondering how I was going to find my family, I heard a soft voice next to me. The kind woman said that God had given her a verse for me when I had walked into the chapel hours earlier. I felt myself tighten up to guard my spirit once again from some cruel, religious, trite one-liner. I never once turned my head to even acknowledge her presence. My heart felt calloused and unreachable. She said, "God told me to have you read Psalm 56." I doubted it was God because at least He knew my blindness prevented me from reading! Reluctant to face my new, unwelcome counselor but sensing that she was about to leave, I turned to her and asked, "Could you please read it to me?" The words she read penetrated my soul. "Lord, you saw me tossing and turning in the night and every tear I have ever cried you have kept in your bottle. But when I called on the name of the Lord the tide was turned and all my enemies began to flee, for this one thing I know, you are for me." After all, my Father did know where I was. He had been close enough to catch my every tear. Perhaps the darkness I felt was merely the shadow of His wings. I was being hidden in his pavilion that protected me in the midst of every tumultuous storm that had come. He had promised, "He would be near to all who called to Him." I had been found at last.

This passage reignited my passion to know a Father who would care to catch every tear I had ever cried. My mind searched scripture for a starting place. I knew that His love was steadfast and His mercies new every morning. I thought about the forgiveness He extends as far as the East is from the West. I remembered hearing a verse somewhere in Jeremiah stating that the Lord has a future and a hope for His children. It soothed me to know that God is love, and darkness is not in Him. He promised that His hand was not too short to reach nor His ear deaf toward us. The scriptures washed over me with a fresh, fragrant cleansing.

The Prince of Peace, Jesus, filled the room with His calming and deep, abiding peace that passed all that I could understand. My open heart was free of all defenses and longed to be held by His nail-scarred hands. He had been touched by my infirmity, and we were partakers of pain and suffering together. My pain was minimized as I focused on the magnitude of His sacrifice. The Savior of my soul embraced me, understanding my deepest, questioning pain.

His tenderness was a far cry from the insensitive, religious comments of misguided Christians. His acceptance negated others' disapproval. His comforting presence filled me with hope as I heard Him offer His grace to me. I no longer cared about my condemners, knowing that He stood by my side reassuring me that I could build on His faith. My fears were quieted as I placed my hand in His. I inquired, "Do you have any use for me?"

CHAPTER SIXTEEN
SEEING BEYOND PARENTING

In spite of the challenges, near mishaps, and humorous events that come with it, there is no greater calling than that of a mother. God had made it clear that He wanted to use me in that role and I loved my little trio.

The sisters were very unique in their approaches to life. Anna was always the one who was the most serious, cautious, and compliant. Lindey, on the other hand, was the social, artistic child who was always fashionable. From the moment she could speak, Lindey told us what color she looked best in and how she wanted her hair fixed. Holly, with her strong will and competitive drive, tried to keep up with her older sisters. It wasn't until years later that I learned how much Holly's sisters encouraged her to do naughty things and blamed her for everything. Anna was quiet, Lindey was extremely funny, and Holly was the mastermind.

From an early age, the girls were beginning to express personality traits that I believe were preordained. Mercy motivated Anna. Her kind heart was always tender to others and the Lord. She served everyone. Lindey studied classical ballet from the age of four and always seemed to float into any room with graceful beauty. Her administrative skills facilitated her role as a delegator. In short, she told her sisters where to be and what to do. Holly mirrored her mother's prophetic ways and only held two crayons in her coloring box—black and white. Also, like her mother, she valued her independence; we often found Holly tucked away in her favorite tree. Holly and Lindey, only twenty months apart, bonded like twins. Anna, three and one-half years older than Lindey, mothered the two.

I have always been passionate about making a memory each day. I became the family photographer to make sure that all the "Kodak moments" were captured for viewing later. Granted, many of our pictures were of people without heads. My photographic obsession is motivated by my hope that one day I will be healed and able to see what I have missed through the years. No matter how well I compensated for my loss, it pierced my heart not to see clearly the beautiful faces of my children. I only wept in private because I spent each new day living life to the fullest.

Shopping trips were stressful, and I would demand that the girls stay close to me. Usually, Tony or a friend would drop us off at the mall, leaving us on our own. One particular afternoon I was looking at something in a store when the children were acting rowdy. Long after my patience had worn thin, I turned to my side and sternly said, "Knock it off now or we will go home immediately. Do you hear me?" To my alarm, I heard my children say, "Yes, Mom. We're right here behind you." I had just corrected someone else's children, and I sure hoped they were not standing with their parents.

On another shopping trip with Anna, she played in the clothes rack, hiding in the center as many small children do. Many minutes had passed before I realized that she had taken her hiding game too far. I had everyone in the store looking for my missing child. Finally, with my heart racing, I stepped into the mall in search of my firstborn, even though I actually did not have the ability to see her clearly. Several people who recognized me from our weekly television program offered to help me find my wandering lamb. I managed to call Tony, informing him I had misplaced Anna. As he sped to rescue us, I paced the mall to find our preschooler. Anna had strolled the length of the mall to the toy store. There she stood, holding the hand of a little boy her size and age. They had never met, but they paused together outside the store to peek in at the toys. Anna looked as if she were on her first date with a young man. When I called her name, she said, "Hi, Mommy." I hugged her tightly, not knowing whether to punish her or kiss her incessantly.

When Lindey was four years old and attending our church preschool, she had a little friend with whom she became enamored. She loved how her friend and her mother would always drive to shopping malls and restaurants together. Lindey was also impressed with this only child's wardrobe and fashionable shoes. Without any discussion or warning, Lindey decided that her friend's mother was more appealing than her own because of all the places she could drive.

It was near suppertime one evening when Lindey struggled down the steps with a large suitcase. I met her at the base of the steps and said, "Where are you going? Are you running away from home?" She said, "Yes, I am going to live with my friend." Playing along with what I thought was a silly pretend game I said, "Well, we will miss you." Continuing, I asked, "May I look in your suitcase to see what all you are taking with you?" She promptly opened her bright red suitcase and showed me her five pairs of underwear and her three pairs of shoes. By this time, the whole family had gathered around her suitcase and tried to figure out why she wanted to leave us. I joined the pretend game as I asked Tony if he would drive her to her new home. He pulled his keys out, as Lindey went to gather her coat. My eyes began to well with tears as I felt the innocent rejection of my young daughter, knowing that her little game was becoming quite serious. Anna, now seven years old, quietly observed the conflict and she too had become disturbed. She firmly requested that Lindey follow her to the family room. We could hear Anna begin her motherly lecture as she said, "Lindey, sit down! This all began with Adam and Eve." It only took a few moments for Lindey to change her mind and decide to stay with her original family. I am convinced to this day that Lindey was afraid Anna might take her from Genesis to the end of the Bible as she tried to convince Lindey of her wrong decision and hurtful ways. I was relieved to have Lindey unpack, but I could not help but wonder how many other mothers she envied because they could drive.

Keeping my eye on the children was definitely a challenge. I knew other mothers with perfect eyesight who had stories of their children getting away from their watchful eyes, too, but I still felt incredibly inferior for being a sightless mother.

One afternoon I was working in the house when the doorbell rang. The children had been outside playing, and Holly was in the back yard on the swing set, or so I thought. When I answered the door, a truck driver inquired, "Ma'am, is this your little girl?" There Holly stood, holding the truck driver's hand, looking as if she were inquiring, too. He informed me that he had been to every door in the neighborhood because he had found Holly playing near a busy main street. The fear of what could have happened nauseated me. Keeping an eye on the children was definitely a challenge. I knew other mothers with perfect eyesight who had stories of their children getting away from their watchful eyes, too, but I still felt incredibly inferior for being a sightless mother.

Though there were a few times when my lack of eyesight was dangerous for all of us, for the most part we learned to work together. The buddy system became imperative, not only for the girls' looking out for each other, but also for their looking out for me. Our special reading times would be as a family with Daddy reading and the girls turning the pages as I listened, too. In the moments when I was tempted to feel sorry for my daughters because of the extra burden they carried, I would reassure myself that, in time, they would have an advantage in life. Our children had learned to serve and be watchful for others. The family had to communicate with words and not just point and nod. They had worked through difficult challenges, and the result was that they were part of a very close life-support team.

I loved to take my children one by one on outings. One day, it was Holly's turn to go to the mall with me for lunch. We perched ourselves in an open balcony restaurant at a table with an excellent view, just as I had requested. When our waitress came with the menus, I asked what the special of the day was. She pointed to it. Trying to protect our images and not expose the fact that neither Holly nor I could read, I asked, "What kind of sandwiches do you have?" She once again pointed to the list on the menu. Holly and I looked at each other and smiled, "We would like two of your best hamburgers, please." Neither of us was interested in parading our limitations to the world; we just wanted to order our lunch.

It is amazing what even a blind mother can see, however. My children always thought I had eyes in the back of my head—eyes with perfect 20/20 vision. I could see a wrong attitude clearly, and I could sense if a room was cluttered or orderly. I learned to ask many questions.

Our lives were filled with activities, but the central focus was the church. Teenage babysitters often watched the children while Tony and I stayed busy with our ministry responsibilities. We included our children in some ministry outings and special events, and they occasionally appeared on our weekly television show. Viewers loved them, but it took us days to get over the exhaustion of keeping up with our special guests.

Our family delighted in being used by the Lord to demonstrate His mercy and power. Each winter I was asked to sing at a large Christian convention hosted by our city. I can remember bringing Anna as a very young child up to the platform with me and placing her on a chair as she spoke the blessing of Numbers 6:24-26 to more than a thousand people. A hush fell over the audience as she began to say, "The Lord bless you and keep you; the Lord make His face to shine upon you, and be gracious unto you." Tears welled up in the eyes of many as she continued, "The Lord lift up His countenance upon you, and give you peace." They remembered praying for this little girl when she hovered between life and death. The scripture we prayed over Anna during those days of crisis, "You shall live and not die, and declare what God has done forever," was being fulfilled in front of this large crowd of people.

One spring evening, Tony and I sat on our front porch, watching our miracle daughters play in the neighborhood. As they ran laughing, full of energy and life, we sat, feeling the opposite. Tony was looking through the mail when I remarked, "I'm empty and need some time away." Tony continued to shuffle through the pile of mail as he agreed with my cry and said, "Yes, and where shall we go?"

We both needed a season of refreshing and a change of atmosphere. We loved all that we were a part of, yet we wondered if the reason we felt exhausted and empty was because we had not paced ourselves wisely. Our physical battles and challenges alone would have been enough to weary the most experienced, decorated soldier. Surely we would qualify for several medals of honor and three purple hearts for the battles now chronicled in our history.

Tony pulled from the stack of mail a brochure advertising an upcoming seminar that seemed like a perfect match for what we needed. Its emphasis was on life principles, character building, effective homes, and ministry. Without hesitation, we decided to attend this weeklong conference in Atlanta, Georgia.

God prepared the incredible arrangements needed for us to find rest and a renewed focus on loving the Savior. Through a strange string of events, God gave us a palatial, two-story house to stay in for free, and my parents kept the children. At the conference we were merely two people in the midst of 15,000. Though we were insignificant in the crowd of people, we felt that God had orchestrated the seminar just for the two of us. We sat riveted to our seats, oblivious to the passing hours. God had intervened in our life-dreams, goals, and view of ministry, and began to share His priorities with us. He had our full attention and receptive hearts. Our blinded eyes were being opened.

After returning home, we reordered the direction of our family and ministry. Everything changed. Instead of simply managing our children and teaching them to be well behaved, we began to value their potential for the generations to come. God was fulfilling the scriptures in Psalms 127 and 128: "Children are like arrows in the hands of a mighty warrior." We realized that our children and their children and their children would touch far-reaching parts of the world beyond our life spans. The heart of God was that our entire household would serve Him, no matter what the age. Tony and I saw not only our responsibilities in training our children in the ways of God, but also our purpose in living for His purposes.

As a household, we began to develop a life-message. Each day we would look into the Word of God, memorize scriptures, and discuss the day's events from a Biblical view, discerning wisdom and truth. The cry of our hearts was for our children to know the Savior and that it not be just an academic, Sunday School understanding. Our goal was to see our children become strong and mighty in spirit for His glory. We no longer looked at our children as a dutiful responsibility until they left home for college but, instead, devoted our lives to training, molding, and sharpening them in Christ.

We made the difficult decision to home-educate, even though we were the founders and overseers of a Christian school. Together, Tony and I joined in straightening our little arrows, sharpening their points, and placing the fletching in order. Under the guidance of the Lord, we wanted our children to be able to hit the target of God's goal and make a bull's eye. We welcomed being refined like silver and gold.

It was no longer Tony and I who worked hard to help other families, but our prayer became for our whole household to touch the lives of other households. We desired that our lives would be like salt blocks that would cause others to thirst for more of Him. We quickly realized that if our household was strong, then we could inspire other households more successfully. Our paradigm shifted in our drive for ministry. Instead of looking for ministry, we confidently accepted the fact that we were ministry.

We delighted in the times when the Lord called us to minister as a household. I began to teach the girls how to harmonize. I was confident that, if they could make a simple chord, then one day soon they would make rich, lush chords, capturing smooth, family-blended sounds. Lindey continued classical ballet training and added to it sign language as she learned to interpret and communicate the message of the gospel in music and dance. The girls learned large portions of scripture, acting it out and sharing it with literally thousands of people. Our team had become more focused on the potential of working together and growing in Him.

I still dealt with days of frustration, interwoven with sadness, over not being able to see, but I soon realized that my "vision" was keen. Having vision now became my driving force and passion. I was clothed in a new sense of strength and destiny. Life seemed good—or so I thought.

Late one night I stumbled onto Tony crying. He had always been our anchor and steady force in each storm. I wondered if an insensitive church member had unnecessarily criticized him that week, or if he was emotionally burned out. When I asked him why the tears, he remained vague and quickly changed the subject. Several nights later, I saw him wipe the tears from his face as we sat down to eat dinner with the family. Granted, I may not have served his favorite meal that night, but there was no reason for tears. "Why are you crying?" I again inquired. Once more, he absorbed his sadness as we bowed for the dinner prayer. My mind and heart were unsettled. Why the tears? Why now?

CHAPTER SEVENTEEN
SEEING BEYOND
THE EMPTY CHAIR

Excitement filled the air as my daughters carefully set the table in our formal dining room with all of our fine china. The morning events included a special family breakfast. All five members of our McWilliams household owned their own special china pieces. Fine china had been the tool God had used to help me teach our daughters about purity.

I had previously taken each girl to a secret luncheon, one at a time, to explain to her how her life was like fine china that the King had set apart for His special treasure. At the luncheon, I had admonished each young lady to walk in purity as she guarded her heart until the day God would send her man of valor. After the luncheon, I escorted my daughter to the finest china shop in our city and asked her to pick a cup and saucer of her choice to mark this significant event.

I was amazed when the girls picked the same make of china. However, the girls selected different patterns that expressed their unique and delightful personalities. I asked each daughter not to tell her sisters where we had gone or unwrap the fine china for anyone to see until a designated day yet to be announced. Each agreed with a smile of intrigue and excitement.

The special breakfast was the designated day, and I invited each girl to bring her beautifully wrapped gift to be opened for all to see.

The table was set with my china, which my grandmother had given me. The girls came to the dining room table with their precious treasures as we decorated the table with their wrapped gifts.

After breakfast, we asked each one, beginning with the oldest, to unwrap the china she had selected. With each opened box we "oohed" and "aahed" as we admired the symbols that represented their hearts of purity. I served a brewed batch of hot tea, pouring it into each unique china cup and saucer. We reminded our daughters that they were like fine china, set apart for the King's special service. They were not plain and ordinary but, instead, were fragile and valuable with ornate handcrafting treasured by Him. Tony admonished our royal maidens to guard their hearts and minds.

Our routine after breakfast was to open the scriptures and read the Psalms. I was amazed when my husband read the day's passage, "Lord, you are my portion and you have become my cup." We had not planned this reading, but we knew it was not a coincidence. A hush filled our table, as we were aware that the Savior sat with us. We rejoiced as we realized the One who had granted life now assisted us in teaching our young.

In spite of our joy, I continued to notice an ever-growing sadness that would come over my husband from time to time. One night after dinner, I caught him lingering at the table. "What on earth is the problem?" I inquired. He sat still, hesitating to tell me the truth, for he had been avoiding this moment. I remarked, "You might as well tell me because my imagination is going wild." Wiping tears from his eyes, he said, "There are empty chairs at our table." I was half irritated with his answer, asking, "What do you mean?" He repeated his answer and my irritation grew. "What are you talking about?" He then began to tell me that for months he had this growing desire for more children but he feared my reaction. He knew me well. I responded, "If it's the empty chairs at our table that bother you, then I'll remove them in hopes it will cure your sadness."

I felt backed into a corner that I did not like. I remembered the doctors' insisting that our childbearing days end because of the high risk to each baby and the loss of more of my eyesight with each pregnancy. I had embraced the doctors' reports and advice, and my womb was closed, as well as my mind and heart. After all, I did not think it was fair of God to team up with my husband about a matter that would involve my body. Even though I would never have changed our course and my children were my most treasured gifts, I was not interested in putting my life in any more jeopardy. In my mind, the conversation was over and the subject closed for the rest of our marriage. I challenged Tony to simply enjoy our three miracle daughters and be content. Surely, God knew the risk involved with having more children, didn't He?

As my husband's heart became more tender, I hardened mine. He had surprised me with his longing, and I was filled with fear. I felt justified, as I had paid a price to give birth in the first place. I did pray, however: "God, if this is really of you, then you must change my heart, too."

In my fear, I justified building a wall between my husband and God, and me. I felt they had ganged up on me. In many ways, our lives went on as before, or so I tried to pretend. The girls occupied our days, and I continued to serve as the pastor's wife. My husband grieved in private, as he prayed to the Lord for an answer to his puzzling desire for more children.

Tony never tried to talk me into changing my mind, but God softly assured me that I could rest in trust. I am not sure as to exactly when I opened my mind and heart to the Savior. I had already trusted Him with my life, but I said aloud one evening, "I trust you Father." I knew there were two whom I loved and trusted—my Savior and my husband. I resolved to be a modern day Sarah and willingly follow. My thoughts were, "If I die trusting God and my husband, then I am still in good hands." Buried deep below my fear and the doctors' reports was the feeling that I, too, wanted more children. One night I told my husband that I explicitly trusted my life in his hands and God's. I was open to being willing.

Even though we had decided to have more children, we still had some obvious obstacles. We had listened to the advice of the doctors years earlier, and my husband had taken the necessary measures to stop any chance of more babies in our home. "How would this problem be solved?" I wondered.

Tony found a list of reversal doctors. But the price tag was costly. Once again, we faced what seemed like an impossible situation. We decided to pick a doctor and simply ask the Lord for the money. After all, if this were His leading, then it would also be His provision. Tony was drawn to one particular doctor in Texas. This seemed ridiculous to me since another reversal doctor was only three hours away instead of twenty-two. We inquired of both, but Tony felt strongly that he should use the doctor in Texas. We asked the Lord once again to make a way where there seemed to be none.

Within a few days, we opened the mail and held a check from the IRS for the exact amount of money we needed for the surgery. I began to jump up and down at the quick provision of the Lord. I also sensed His confirmation to what others might view as being a dangerous and needless quest. My husband did not share my excitement, telling me, "Gail, the IRS has made a mistake on our tax return." I could not believe him. "What on earth do you mean?" He explained that the IRS had incorrectly figured his pastor's allowance and ministerial deductions, and we needed to put the money in savings until we knew for sure it was our money to spend. He immediately called our accountant, and she confirmed that Tony was correct and the money should be sent back. I could not believe the turn of events.

Within a few months, I received a call to speak at a conference in California. This was my second invitation to minister in central California. I had previously stated that, if ever I were asked to speak there, I wanted to drive out and use it as a long, eventful field trip for our home-educated girls. I made the arrangement with my sponsoring church that we would be driving, and they could send airfare money, but we would use it for gas. We planned a three-week trip with ministry in the middle. Since we were traveling across the country, we decided a stop in Texas would be feasible, though it was twelve hours out of the way. We made arrangements to see the west coast and then to stop on our way back to keep our reversal appointment with the doctor of Tony's choice. The trip was filled with great memories and outstanding excursions. The Grand Canyon, Yosemite, San Francisco Bay, and other famous sights filled the days when we were not ministering.

After two weeks of driving, sightseeing, and ministry presentations, we finally arrived in Texas near San Antonio. All five of us went to the clinic because they encouraged families to come together. Our children were to wait in a special room with a video that would last the length of the surgery. When the doctor came to talk with us, he asked if he could take a picture, saying, "This new baby is going to need a good family." We all smiled, except for my nervous husband. Then the doctor asked me to accompany my husband into the surgery room. Wow. This was a change of events. Usually, he was the one escorting me to the surgery table.

The girls were happy in their private theater, and I walked with the nurse to the operating suite. Tony was comfortable because he already felt the effects of the medication. My stomach was now queasy, and I would have welcomed some calming drugs, too.

However, the soft lighting and melodious Christian music in the room created a calming mood. Someone asked me to sit at my husband's head so I could give him support and watch a monitor. Did someone forget to remind the doctor that I was visually challenged? I pretended to watch the monitor while I listened closely to every sound. With a groggy husband, the surgery began. The doctor was kind, and we talked away as he worked on the man I loved. During our conversation, he told me that he had just undergone eye surgery himself. "Oh brother," I thought. "Two blind mice working to restore my husband's original plumbing." About that time, the monitor I was watching sounded an alarm, a monotone similar to what I had heard on television medical dramas. Would someone be crying out "code blue" next? Had I overlooked some major reading on the monitor, and now my husband was dead? I cried to the nurse, "Help. There's something terribly wrong." Neither the doctor nor nurse answered immediately because they were busy cutting and sewing. Soon, they assured me that the monitor was simply malfunctioning and everything was fine. But I was not fine. I was rattled and ready to have my husband back. The doctor was hopeful but said that it would take some time to see if the surgery worked.

Tony began to stir as they rolled him into a recovery room. Like clockwork, the girls had finished their movie and my husband was back on his feet, while I was pale and had to sit down for a moment. Astonishingly, within the hour we all were celebrating at McDonalds in this small, southwestern town. It was Lindey's ninth birthday. The surgeon's wife went with us, as we had become friends from all the previous correspondence. By that afternoon we were at the Alamo. Understandably, Tony's pace was slower than ours; nevertheless, he saw the sights with us and tried to add historical information to our students' school field trip. Science and history were covered thoroughly during that eventful day in March.

Within three short months, we were expecting a baby. Two surgeries had certainly been successful—Tony's and the attending doctor's eye surgery. Our reversal baby was on the way.

CHAPTER EIGHTEEN
SEEING BEYOND THE LOSS

We had obeyed, and, although what we had done seemed ridiculous to some, we had opened our lives to receive one more child. As we were in touch with the Father's heart, we saw the fruit of our decision.

Some of the fondest memories of parenting were during this time in our lives. Our daughters willingly followed our lead as we trained them in character, home schooling, and pursuing God. We had their hearts, and they had ours.

I have always enjoyed making a memory, finding unique ways to enjoy the journey. One night I planned a special outing. The girls would answer riddles with the promise of a campout at the end.

One clue led us to a nearby park, then to an ice cream shop. The next clue was more difficult as it led us to the edge of town where Abraham Lincoln once lived along the Sangamon River. We toured his small cabin and discussed his diligence and work ethic as God groomed him to be a leader. By the time we started back to the car, the girls had already figured out our next clue that would lead us to play miniature golf by the lake.

We were driving down the country road to our next destination when Tony spotted a house with flames shooting from the roof. All of a sudden we sped down the road. I could not imagine why all the rush to simply play a game of golf. "What are you doing?" He exclaimed that we were headed to a burning house to see if the residents were aware they were at risk.

As we had pulled onto the farm property, Tony jumped out of the car, and ran toward the burning house. We watched with fright as he pounded on the door, yelling, "Anyone here? Is anyone home?" Without success, he tried to knock the door down. Unfortunately, what looked easy in a Hollywood movie was vastly different in real life. We ladies sat in the car, watching our own show of intense drama and horror.

Knowing he was racing against time, Tony sprinted swiftly to the front of the house. This door was unlocked, but because this entrance was not used, a couch blocked the way. Tony forcibly shoved the door open and rushed into the burning house, yelling for anyone who might need rescuing. Meanwhile, the girls cried with fright, and I prayed fervently. From our front row seat, we watched the fire as it crept down the side of the house, spreading quickly. "Tony, hurry!" I yelled. No one heard our screams.

Tony found no one at home but knew the fire would consume the entire house and its contents if something weren't done. He located a phone in the kitchen and dialed 911. The emergency dispatcher calmly asked for an address. Tony franticly shuffled through the nearby stack of mail and was able to give the address and rural route. Then the woman put Tony on hold. What part of "burning house" had she not understood?

When she returned, she excitedly instructed Tony to get out of the house. The girls and I shouted with relief at the first sight of our superman. Running from the house, Tony raced to find some kind of water hose. Unfortunately, the only source of water to be found was a hog trough with one rusty bucket lying near it. Grabbing the bucket and scooping up water, he began throwing it on the burning house. From his new position, this one-man rescue operation discovered the cause of the flames. A live electrical wire had snapped from its connection at the house and, undoubtedly, had started the fire. The girls and I prayed for Tony to get back to the car. When he saw a propane tank not far from the house, he jumped in the car to drive his terrified family to safety. A back row seat for this ongoing drama was a welcome change.

We listened for the sirens of the fire trucks, knowing the tall, ripe corn in the fields could make it difficult to find us. We stood in the middle of the road, flagging them down. Within minutes, a crowd of people had come to help, along with the residents who had been notified of the fire. Furniture and belongings were carried out of the house that now was only smoking. The fire was extinguished. As we drove away, one of the girls said, "Mommy, did you plan that, too?"

Later, we heard that the house reignited in the night and burned to the ground. The owner's belongings were saved, and all of their livestock was safe due to Tony's heroic attempts.

We were finally able to continue our treasure hunt. The last clue took us to our inviting campsite for the night. We had circled the county making memories for a lifetime, only to arrive back in our own driveway. Confused, the girls said, "I thought we were going camping?" They had forgotten that before we had set out on our adventure, I had run back into the house for "one more thing." While in the house, I had placed sleeping bags on the family room floor. I brought the dining room chairs in and draped covers over them for makeshift tents and added flashlights and candles for the full effect of our camping adventure. Our campfire for the night had already been provided. My designed treasure hunt had an unforgettable outcome. One thing, for sure, was that the girls' daddy was a hero in their eyes.

Tony had also become a bigger hero in my life, too. His unrelenting faith and obedience before God moved me to follow his example. As we grew in trusting Him, my womb began to grow with new life. We waited to tell our congregation our good news until the end of my first trimester, when the baby within was securely planted and growing. We knew they would be shocked because everyone thought our family was complete. After all, Anna was thirteen, Lindey, nine and Holly, seven. Since our family often sang together, we worked up a song with the grand finale being our shouting, "And we are having a baby!" It was a moving production, but the congregation sat in silence, stunned at our news. Finally, the silence was broken by nervous applause. We were so thrilled that we didn't even notice the skeptics.

A few days after our announcement, I was heartsick when I began to bleed and cramp. "How could this be?" I thought. We have already paid the price for this precious, wanted child. The doctors prescribed bed rest and I willingly agreed.

I felt helpless lying perfectly still in bed, hoping I would not disturb my endangered, unborn baby. I pleadingly told my little one, "Please, hang on securely to me."

One afternoon, I cried out to the Lord, "Jesus, be near to me." Words cannot fully explain the next event. I literally felt hands enter my stomach and womb. Just as quickly as they had entered, they were removed. I began to worship the Lord, for I knew it must be His hands. The Great Physician had come to make a house call, and He had touched my unborn child. I was filled with hope.

However, within hours, the bleeding and cramping had increased significantly. Tony and I quickly left for the hospital. My parents had moved three hours north of us, so we had called a friend to watch our daughters as they slept in the late night.

Once more, Tony drove the familiar road to the high-risk hospital. I lay in the back of the van, with towels soaking up the flow of blood. This was not what we expected. God had put the desire for more children into both of us, yet we faced death one more time.

I was examined in the emergency room and was in unbearable pain on the gurney when the doctor finally arrived. He was not my primary obstetrician, but we had met before in the office. He was a Christian man and usually kind, but not tonight. He came into the room visibly upset and scolded me for waiting so long. I rose off the bed to partially sit up and crossly asked him, "Are you here to condemn me or to help me, Doctor?" As I lay back down on the blood soaked gurney, he replied, "Yes, I will help you."

The rest is still a blur as they rolled me into surgery for a D&C. The only people who knew of our midnight crisis were the director of our school and the young woman watching our children. I had specifically asked the director not to notify my parents until morning because I didn't want them to worry. She agreed, but she did not keep her word. On our way to the hospital, she had phoned my parents. They immediately left to join us.

After the surgery and hours before dawn, I found myself free of the bleeding and cramping, but the pain in my heart had just begun. I lay on my side sobbing, trying to make sense of the last year's journey and following the Lord's leading. As I cried, I felt a soft hand on my shoulder. I knew it was my mother. How good it was to have her at my side as I groped for comfort. Tony sat quietly with my dad, groping for answers too. If Tony did not already feel guilty, others made him feel responsible. After all, they blamed him for his decision to have more children.

Just hours after my surgery, Tony returned to preach to our church. He was a broken man who stood transparent before his congregation. Had it only been one week earlier that we had shared our good news? How sad it was to deliver this news of great loss.

I will never understand people and their insensitivity in times of sorrow. Some families had decided that they were going to leave the church to start their own church, and they chose to tell Tony about their plans after the service. Our mourning had only just begun.

In less than 24 hours, I had returned home empty. The loss of our child and the news of church members leaving left me in depression. In spite of all I had been through, I had never tasted defeat like this. I had lost my hope. I had lost my vision. I had lost my respect for people. I had lost my strength to get back up and fight. I had lost time with the girls. I do not even remember who cared for them. I also had lost my desire to obey God. Was this to be the result of our obedience to Him? I felt lost.

My only comfort was thinking about those loving hands that had come into my womb the previous afternoon. I pondered that special moment. I knew now that the Lord Himself had ushered my unborn child to His perfect home. I cannot explain what had happened that afternoon; however, I knew He had come. In time, I would fully trust Him again; but for now, I numbed my broken heart so that I could survive the deep pain and loss.

CHAPTER NINETEEN
SEEING BEYOND DEPRESSION

Melancholy days followed. We had never dreamed that our obedience would lead to heartache. I searched for answers to understand why we lost our baby. We would never have desired more children if the Father had not given us the desire first. Surely He knew the risk. The reversal surgery had been perfect and a miracle baby had been on the way. What had happened?

People tried to say encouraging things, hoping I would swiftly pass through the grieving stages. I could not comfort my husband because I could not comfort myself. I knew that three little ladies needed me, but I could not pick myself up and find my stride because I had decided to sit down. I did not want to care anymore.

I felt betrayed. What kind of husband would put his wife in such physical and emotional danger? I also felt betrayed by my own body as I suffered the pressure of knowing my biological clock was running out. Did I even want more children? I couldn't even see the faces of the children I already had. More than any other struggle was my overwhelming feeling that God had betrayed me. My life had been built on loving Him and wanting to please Him. Now I questioned why had we gone to the expense and bother of having another child if we were to lose it in the end.

Because I could not answer these questions, I focused on yet another betrayal. What kind of people would leave the church and us in the middle of our personal tragedy? After all, we had stood with them in the midst of their own crises time after time. I resented these people. Our Christian school was stronger than the church that had founded it. In the past, I had wondered why so many leaders' wives seemed detached and lonely with self-constructed barbwire around their hearts, hanging a sign for all to read—"No trespassing here!" Now, I understood. I held all that I loved at a distance and learned to mask deep pain by busying myself with various activities at the church and in our Christian school. Darkness resided inside my soul.

Eight months after my miscarriage, Tony and I flew to Texas to attend a pastor's conference in San Antonio. On our commuter flight to Chicago, our seat assignments separated us, and I sat alone. Within my heart I screamed louder than the droning engines. "God, I love you, but it's your people that I cannot stand." Immediately, I heard His response, "Then we have a problem." Instantly, I realized that I was not in harmony with God, the Creator of the universe. I was suddenly aware of my vulnerability in the small plane and I remember thinking, "God, can we talk about this later on the ground?" But even on the ground, I wasn't ready to talk.

The trip away was medicine for us. One of the largest churches in San Antonio hosted the conference, and a limited group of two hundred pastoral leaders from all over the nation attended. Our personal mentors and friends from Georgia were among the speakers, and we looked forward to their hugs and encouragement. We were not disappointed. The conference was designed by a brilliant staff which recognized that pastors do not need to attend seminars all day long but, instead, need enjoyable outings and rest.

It was here that my heart began to deal with the core of my masked pain. I longed to return to the intimate walk I once had with my God. Life without Him was empty. I had replaced Him with the silly thought that I could govern my own affairs and control life. In my attempt not to feel pain or take risks with others, I had ripped off the umbilical cord to my source of life. Each day of the conference, people who made me want to care again surrounded me. In the middle of the laughter, fun, inspiration, and honest talk, I realized that my ability to trust was growing.

One particular afternoon, after stepping forward for prayer at the close of one of the sessions, the senior pastor told Tony, "You cannot fail in God." Again and again, he repeated this as Tony broke. Then he moved to me and, as he began to call on the name of the Lord over me, I cried from my secret, inner part. Deeply embedded pain surfaced. For nearly an hour I cried and released all that I had suppressed, while loving comrades held me in their arms. My soul and heart were purged of hatred, bitterness, and disappointment. I resolved to trust the Master of my life no matter what I could or could not understand. I belonged to Him, and there was no one in life I trusted more. He alone was God, and my time was in His hands. I fully surrendered my heart to His keeping.

God, our Father, had not failed us; we had not failed Him. We remembered Abraham and his son, Isaac. Abraham had waited a lifetime for this promised son; yet when God asked Abraham to sacrifice Isaac's life, he never wavered, knowing the Lord would provide. I resolved in my heart that He who promised is faithful. It became evident that joy was not found in the end result only, but in obeying the Father's voice. We would obey first and understand later. I knew that obedience was greater than any sacrifice.

Later that night, all two hundred of us ate dinner outside on the River Walk. Music, laughter, and fellowship sealed the work of my Father that day. He had repaired my heart.

Depression had been exchanged for a fresh confidence. A verse that permeated my thoughts was, "Why so downcast oh my soul, put your hope in God." Once again, He alone would be my refuge and strength. His view of life reached farther than mine. I could only see the shadows, but He saw the lighted path. He not only could see the immediate, but He also saw the beginning from the end.

I left my depression somewhere in Texas, at the foot of the cross. Much to my wonder, God Himself had tucked away a surprise souvenir as a keepsake that marked our renewed hearts. The gift was to be opened after we got home, handpicked by God. We were pregnant.

CHAPTER TWENTY
SEEING BEYOND
PAIN

I have always said that it has taken a team to have a McWilliams baby. Countless doctor visits, tests, specialists, and hard decisions have bonded us with some of the finest people in the world. Two such men had invited our family to worship with them during the Christmas holidays. All of my doctors were Catholic and open to life. We spent a very special Christmas Eve attending our first Catholic mass with them. I thought it would be a new experience and memory for the family, plus I was interested in their lives as well.

My obstetrician played the guitar during the contemporary worship, and my endocrinologist sat a few rows in front of us. We were unmistakably the only Protestants on the back row. My children were fascinated with the kneeling benches, and they tried to kneel through the whole service. Tony sat at one end, and I sat at the other, with the children between us.

As my eyesight had dimmed, my other senses had become more acute. During the service, this was embarrassing when I began to smell something that alarmed me. I whispered to the child next to me, "Tell the others to tell your dad that something is burning." I placed my hand on my purse and coat, ready for a quick exit if we needed to leave. In loud whispers the girls relayed to me, "Mom, its incense being burned." As I had imagined, we all learned something about how our Catholic friends worshiped—I did, for sure. When we left the cathedral, snow was falling, creating a picturesque Christmas card scene. With only two weeks left in an uncomplicated, perfect pregnancy, I declared aloud, "It is a wonderful life." Daughter four would arrive soon.

Two weeks after Christmas, a familiar team gathered around me at the hospital as I anticipated the birthing of a new chapter. A nurse told me to sit up and bend over as far as I could. This was difficult because my belly was great with a nearly full-term little girl awaiting her debut. Bending at my waist seemed nearly impossible. The anesthesiologist waited impatiently, anxious to place his needle and the epidural tubing deep into my lower back.

I was very familiar with the cesarean procedure. In a few moments I would be medicated so I wouldn't feel the sharpened knife in the doctor's skilled hands. The presiding surgeon was the fourth obstetrician from the faithful medical team that had cared for me for over eleven years. We had become close to our doctors as a result of all the specialized care and frequent visits. Everyone was pulling for us to have one more miracle baby. The doctor and his wife were expecting at nearly the same time; however, we were ten years their senior.

I was finally directed to lie down as everyone took positions in the surgery room on this Tuesday morning in January. Tony sat at my head while I was wired for sound. An oxygen mask was placed over my face, and I was strapped to the table. Both arms were fixed to boards and connected to essential monitors. I studied the ceiling while listening to the team's many instructions. However, something did not seem right.

The doctor asked if I was numb, but I could still feel his hands on my belly. I was helped to a sitting position as the anesthesiologist placed another needle in my back. This happened four times until the medication finally took effect. Later, I was told that I not only was given an epidural but also a spinal.

Within minutes our fourth daughter was lifted from my womb, allowing my lungs room to expand and, letting me breathe with ease again. Immediately, I heard a little cry from our newest gift. She was healthy and normal with a perfect APGAR score.

As I listened to the busy activity of those caring for our newborn, I knew I had waited long enough. "There's something wrong," I told them, "I've been through this before and my back should not be hurting like this!" No one answered me so I stated again, "Something is not right in my back; I can feel everything." Because I was only able to stare at the ceiling, I could not see my medical team making eye contact with one another. The nurses knew I should not be feeling any pain. In fact, the joy of having a cesarean section and a good anesthesiologist is to have just the right amount of medication to get through the most painful hours in order to enjoy the first moments with your baby. Of course, I had never had the privilege of holding my newborns, because one of us was always whisked away so staff could deal with our medical problems.

In spite of the unbelievable pain in my back, I was rolled into recovery. Then to my great surprise, the nurse brought my new miracle bundle and said warmly, "Congratulations, Mommy. She's beautiful!" I forgot the excruciating back pain as I held the only baby I had ever been able to hold immediately after delivery. My little one lay quietly in my arms, content to snuggle as I sang to her. "You Are My Sunshine, My Only Sunshine." The nurses quieted as I sang, and many came by to thank me for the private concert and memorable moment. When I held my new joy, my mind erased the pain of any previous loss. My back, though, would remind me for many months that this child had come with a great price.

We named our daughter Lydia Ellison, a name that I loved. The name Lydia was from the scriptures. Lydia of old was a seller of purple and the first convert to the gospel in Europe. In the Bible, Lydia used her influence and funds to assist the Apostle Paul's work and mission for Christ. Based on her namesake, a seller of purple, there was no doubt as to the color of choice for our little Lydia. She had purple blankets, sleepers, pacifiers, ribbons, and bows. When we arrived home, there were purple balloons outlining the porch and a life-size purple bear on the front door, welcoming our Lady Lydia to the sorority. I announced that in just a few years our daughter could have her own refreshment stand and sell purple Kool-Aid to the neighborhood.

The name Ellison was my great grandfather's sir name. He, too, was the first convert in his family. On his deathbed, he won his neighboring friends to the Lord Jesus Christ. We were reaping the fruit of his decisions, now some four generations later. Our Lydia was commissioned as an infant to carry on her namesakes' faith and live for Christ, making a difference in her generation. No wonder I was not surprised when Lydia, at four years of age, asked if she could take Bibles to all the neighbors. She wanted them to know Jesus.

I was very attached to Lydia and would rarely let the nurses take her from me. I vividly remember the first afternoon after her birthday when she was in my arms, and I softly sang to her. Tony and I were amazed when she turned to look at me. She pulled her head back and tried to focus, as if to say, "Is that what you look like, Mommy? I know your voice." Tony and I immediately bonded with our reversal baby who might never have been. It was a satisfying feeling for both of us, and the fruit of obedience was worth the wait.

My back continued to be racked with painful spasms. The nurses confided that they knew there was talk about the anesthesiologist's mistake and carelessness with my back during the cesarean section. Unfortunately, they told me, I was one of many victims who let this man go unchecked. The observant nurses encouraged me to speak up, and I did. Every drug used to ease the pain was ineffective. Finally, my attending caregiver came up with an unorthodox plan that worked. Late at night, she brought me a wet towel tucked inside a garbage can liner. She had warmed it in the microwave to make it hot and steamy and then placed it on my back to help relieve the pain. She cautioned that I could not let the doctors see her treatment. I was grateful for any relief to the constant, driving pain. I was still convinced that something had gone terribly wrong with my medication, so I insisted on seeing the anesthesiologist.

Medical staff has always considered me to be a compliant patient; I cooperate, and I willingly do what I am told. Therefore, to have a medical "expert" who did not even listen to my complaint was most irritating. The anesthesiologist's disdain of women and his rudeness were appalling. He quickly wrote a prescription but told me that my symptoms were all psychosomatic and that I should just focus on my baby. I felt helpless to fight back because he wore the white coat.

I was given the pain medication he ordered, and within hours, was talking to people who did not exist. I saw spiders crawling everywhere on the walls, and I barely recognized my husband who had not left my side. In spite of the invisible intruders that only I saw, my back continued to ache and throb. The thievery of it all was that I could scarcely experience the joy of my baby.

The morning finally arrived when Lydia and I were released from the hospital. It was a historic day that the entire state would take notice of because the wind chill factor was sixty degrees BELOW zero. Lady Lydia was bundled in all layers of purple as the mother-daughter team awaited our taxi. The night before Lydia's birth, our family was given a new Ford Château van. It was beautiful and roomy for Tony's houseful of girls. Snow covered the ground, and life stood frozen that winter morning. Weathermen warned that no one should go outside except for an emergency. We were willing to leave the warmth of the hospital so our family could be together. I will never understand why I refused the pain pill and muscle relaxer the nurses offered for my back. By the time we arrived at our home nearly one hour away, I was in excruciating pain. I remember walking through the door and handing the baby to my mother, who had come to help. The other girls peeked at their tiny sister. My mother and Tony gave orders for me to go to bed; they would care for our new arrival. That became the procedure for the next few months. I only held Lydia at feeding times. Otherwise, I had to take a number and stand in line like everyone else to hold our long-awaited gift. Oh my, this baby was about to have too many mommas.

It seems odd to me that the world has preconceived ideas about life and families. My mother had bemoaned the fact that she and Dad would probably never know Lydia as they had known the other girls because they were older. Lydia is now a young adult, and my parents are still living. Others expressed regret that because of the large age gap, the older girls would not really know their little sister. Nonsense. They have been an integral part of the team raising Lydia, and all of the sisters are close. Family ties are expressed in the life-values that are embraced. We placed family life as a top priority, and our closeness was not in our ages or common interests but in the fact that God had placed a destiny and call on each of our lives. We were a family that the doctors had said could never be.

Every chair around our dining room table was filled now. We all took our places at our first dinner together. Lydia sat in her car seat at the table with us, as my mother served the traditional homecoming menu—grandmother's roast and mashed potatoes. God had been good to our family. My husband sat with his daughters, like Philip of the scriptures. Philip's daughters were in touch with the heart of their God, and they spoke prophetically in their generation. The process of sculpting our daughters in the palace style was more desired than ever before. We knew that we would need the hand of the Great Architect and His plans to accomplish this successfully in the days and years to come.

CHAPTER TWENTY-ONE
SEEING BEYOND
THE LAUGHTER

Does the prayer of a child reach the Father's ears? What if you are unaware of what they are asking? Well, I am living proof that even a child can search out the heart of the Father as well as express her own desire.

Life had become a manageable routine with more than enough "mothers" in the bunch. I had to issue weekly reminders that I was the original mother of our new little girl, Lydia. She had greater status than a family pet, and, of course, she was more real than a baby doll to her sisters who watched over her every move. The girls laid down their dolls and picked up Lydia for early training in motherhood. The greatest joy is that they were doing a splendid job. At the time, Anna was fourteen, Lindey ten, and Holly nine.

I am not even sure what prompted me to think about more children because I was confident Lydia had been our last. Possibly, it was the early morning nausea that I felt. I never had experienced morning sickness with any of my children. In fact, I felt my very best when I was pregnant. I had more enthusiasm about taking care of myself because someone else was dependent on me. However, I did not feel very good in the mornings, and my queasiness was a daily event.

Early one morning, I decided to surreptitiously find out if there was any possibility that I might be pregnant once again. I had planned to use an extra home pregnancy kit and answer my own haunting question. The only problem was that I did not want my husband to know. It was two months until his birthday and because my love language is gift giving, I thought this would make a great surprise gift—if he were sitting down.

I found Lindey in the upstairs hallway, so I asked her to be my accomplice. I needed extra eyes to pull off this surprise. Lindey's face brightened when the test clearly showed that I was pregnant again. She now felt at liberty to share her own secret with me. "Mom, I have been praying for a little brother for months." Smiling, yet increasingly nauseated, I replied, "Shouldn't you have warned me first?" God had heard her prayers for a baby; however, the odds for a boy were slim to none.

Lindey and I made a pact not to tell anyone else our secret. Our plan was perfect, until about three weeks into the newly discovered pregnancy when I began to bleed—a sign of miscarriage. Everyone else was in bed as Lindey and I met late in the night in the hallway to talk and pray. Lindey sat with her knees curled up and her face buried in her arms as she began to cry. Sitting on the floor beside my little prayer warrior, I leaned over and held her. "Lindey, God has answered your prayers so far. Let's ask Him to keep this baby safe." Together we prayed, agreeing that God could do the impossible. I was tempted to tell Tony about the secret we had been keeping from him, yet I was hopeful that this would be a greater surprise of victory if we could just hold on. So, Lindey and I waited.

One afternoon, I was in my bedroom when a song came on the radio that captured my heart. It was the old spiritual, "His Eye is On the Sparrow". The words refreshed my anxious heart—"Jesus is my fortress, my constant friend is He. His eye is on the sparrow and I know He watches me." My heart was comforted and our secret code word for the unborn child at risk would be "Sparrow" from then on.

Incredibly, that song played on the radio through the next several months. It was an old version and not on the top ten charts, but God had become the program manager with His theme once again, "Trust Me."

In late summer, Tony and I took a trip with some business associates to a rally in the Southeast. All forty of us shared a chartered bus with cramped quarters. I, too, was cramping along the way and the bleeding had returned. My mind said that I must tell Tony about the battle, yet my heart said to wait a little longer. It was only three weeks until his birthday. After all, I didn't have anything else to give him for a gift. Looking back, I do not know how I kept my secret because I was frightened and feeling miserable, but I was also determined to carry out my surprise. The bleeding eventually stopped, and I knew that our "Sparrow" was in the Savior's hands.

When we returned home, I called the doctor and told him about my symptoms. I then arranged for a friend to take me to the hospital for an official pregnancy test, and my results were positive. I asked the hospital if they would personally call my husband and give him the results. I told them about the secret that my daughter and I had been keeping and the birthday surprise. They took on the project with smiles and a willingness to help. So, on my husband's fortieth birthday, he received the phone call: "Mr. McWilliams, we are calling from the hospital to notify you that your wife is officially pregnant again." Tony said, "Oh, really!" as he looked for a chair to sit down. The wait had been worth the joy and surprise.

Finding the right name for this child became a group project. We searched in the Bible, name books, dictionaries, and anything else we could find to help us. Our biggest challenge was trying to find another girl's name; however, we also looked for a boy's, just in case. We also decided as a family that we would not tell anyone else until we could not hide my pregnancy any longer. So, through the fall I wore many suits with jackets and bulky sweatshirts. We were able to hide our family secret until the last trimester. It was a double blessing because we did not have to entertain everyone's fears and, by the time the word was out, the weeks went by fast.

Our familiar regimen began as we followed the path back to all the specialists. My obstetrician thought I had come back for a yearly checkup until he noticed my big smile. We met each other face to face in the hallway. Shocked, he shook his head in unbelief and said, "Again?" to which I responded, "Yes, we're pregnant, and how about you?" He answered, "Yes, us too." Then he proceeded to say, "Let's talk in my office."

Because all my babies have been high-risk, I have had many tests and countless sonograms. For my fifth baby, the sonogram was especially important to me. My doctors and lab techs thought I was overly curious, but I explained that it was a great deal more serious than that. If, by some chance, this baby were to be a boy, then we would have to redecorate our entire house. Our house was used to girls, and the colors and bows proved that in nearly every room. No "man" child should be subjected to this horror until he had firmly bonded with his own male identity. Everyone laughed at me, but I was very serious.

On the last scheduled sonogram, I insisted on staying until we found out the gender of this new baby. The technician worked hard to fill my request but to no avail. As she was about to give up her search, she said, "Why don't you lie on your side facing the wall, and let's see if this position will help us solve the mystery." Up to this time, our baby had remained hidden and quite modest.

In time and with great diligence, the technician found the hidden treasure. Lying with my back to the monitor and my head to the wall, I watched my husband as he looked intently at the screen. Abruptly, the tech said, "There it is as big as life." At that moment my husband's face changed into the softest of expressions and tears filled both of our eyes. I exclaimed, "Are you sure?" She then told us she had only been wrong 1% of her career and she was positive. To think, we were having a boy! We could hardly believe the results. A McWilliams baby boy.

We had to return to the waiting room until the doctor could see us. Speechless and giddy, we tried to absorb the news. "A boy? I can't believe it's a boy." When we walked into the crowded waiting room and looked for available seating, the only two chairs left in the place were across from each other. Unexpectedly, we both began to giggle. Without question, we were the oldest people in the room. We laughed like Abraham's Sarah did when angels told her that she would bear a child in her old age. We could not stop giggling. At one point Tony put a magazine in front of his face and I did the same, but our shoulders kept shaking with laughter. A boy.

The news spread rapidly that the McWilliams were expecting their first boy. People asked, "Did you keep having children until you got your boy?" Others would sigh and say, "Good, now you can quit having children because you have your boy." Many could not imagine why anyone would want a big family in our society. To me, all were biased comments with worldly thinking. I was inundated with situations that made me have to defend our "choice" to have a large family. Why did babies threaten the culture so much?

Connor Edison was born on Good Friday, the opening day of spring baseball season. No wonder this is his game of choice. The pregnancy, the delivery, the hospital stay, and the preparation of our home for our new little guy went off exactly as planned. Connor came home from the hospital dressed in a tuxedo sleeper, eager to meet all the new ladies in his life. He was greeted with his first gift—a ball.

Earlier, we had asked our doctor not to circumcise our young man until the eighth day. He looked surprised as he questioned, "Are you Jewish, too?" No, but it only seemed right to follow the plan of old. Following our request, the doctor reserved a private surgical suite on Connor's eighth day for his first ceremonial celebration. When we walked into the surgery unit, our Catholic doctor greeted us with, "Mazel Tov." We, in turn, had brought him a gift bag of kosher dills, bagels, and cream cheese. Everyone laughed, except Connor. As both men tried to comfort him, they knew that he, too, would soon forget the pain of that moment. I had already removed myself because it was too much trauma for this new momma.

Having a son was also a first for the McWilliams extended family, since he was the only grandson on my husband's side. Even when he was very small, we began calling him "Connor Man" as we hoped it would re-enforce his manhood in the midst of all the pink and lace. Before he was born, I had always been partial to girls, and my own daughters were my best friends. Girls seemed to be quieter and able to sit still. However, it did not take long for me to embrace the fact that boys are in training to be men of valor who would be called on to swim the mote, scale the wall, and slay the dragon. I could easily make room for both genders, and I loved the icing God had placed on our already sweet cake. I had, in fact, with the Lord's help, given to my husband an unforgettable birthday gift that would grow more valuable with each passing year.

CHAPTER TWENTY-TWO
SEEING BEYOND DISAPPOINTMENT

During our pilgrimages to doctors, medical students, and research gurus, I encountered a skilled retina specialist. From the moment he stepped into the examining room, I liked him because he reminded me of my brother. On the walls of his patients' examining room hung stories of his successful eye surgeries that had astounded the medical community. When the doctor entered the room and we greeted each other, I quipped, "Hey, Doc, let's make some more history together and add one more testimony to your office wall." In that moment we bonded. After he examined me and studied my medical history, he gave me his diagnosis. Tenderly, he placed his hand on my arm and said, "I'm sorry, Gail. You have fallen through every crack of medical development and research. You are beyond what is now treatable." Feeling great disappointment, I groped for comfort from the Great Physician.

Later that fall, I agreed to surgery that would be performed by another top-ranked retina specialist. The doctor I loved had highly recommended him. The hope and objective was to save one of my eyes from more blindness. Fighting indecision and dread, I agonized for weeks as to what the better choice would be in the long run. Would I stay the course and wait for the miracle touch of my Savior or trust the surgeon's hands under His guidance? Both choices seemed risky, and neither came with a guarantee. I was apprehensive about agreeing to surgery because I knew it would change my life, at least for a season. I would return from the operation with patches on my eyes, which meant total blindness until I was allowed to remove them. My soul searched, asking every hard question and wondering which answer would be the best one.

We decided on the surgery and scheduled an early morning appointment in Chicago several days before Thanksgiving. Before I left home, I asked my children to line up in our family room in their birth order. As I stood in front of them, I held each face in my hands, studying expressions and beauty. I knew that I must imprint their faces in my mind and heart in case I would never "see" them again. I knew my heart could never forget. The pain of that moment, along with the fear of the surgery's possible failure, caused me to linger as I embraced each precious gift of life God had given me.

We spent the night with friends in Chicago so we could be at the hospital early. I studied every tree, car, person, and object that caught my eyes as we traveled and as we walked into the pre-op room. Once again, my trust resided in the One who had made the eyes to see. Trying to calm myself, I listened to the scriptures on my disk player while I waited my turn for the doctor's skilled hands. Soon I was groggy, and within minutes was put into a very deep sleep.

After four hours of intense and complicated surgery, I heard the doctor yelling my name. I remember feeling as if I were in the darkest, black grave, being aroused from my eternal slumber ever so slowly. It was like being lifted from the dark abyss until finally I returned to my body, fully reconnected once more with life's time clock. Where had I been, and what had they done?

Within seconds of being called back to reality, I was flipped to my stomach and told not to move from that position. A gas bubble had been placed in my eye, and my instructions were to lie on my face for the next twenty-one days. There were no promises made or rejoicing that the surgery had been effective. We would have to wait.

The doctor said that the operation was similar to trying to remove chewing gum from a facial tissue and hoping nothing was lost. I wore patches on my eyes and dark glasses. At home, I had to lie on the floor facedown. A friend brought me a most practical and loving gift of lamb's wool for my face to rest on to avoid any possible rug burns. Other friends brought food, but I could not sit up to eat or talk with them. How humbling it was to have everyone chat to my backside.

I used a face cradle that sat inches off the floor to hold my face in place. This is how I stayed, not only while I was awake but also while I slept. This would be my constant position for three weeks. It wasn't until then that I would find out if the surgery had been successful. I reflected on Daniel of the Old Testament and his twenty-one-day cry for help, just as I had when Anna was in the neonatal intensive care unit for the same amount of time. The Lord told Daniel, "I answered you on the first day of your prayer, but it took twenty-one days for the answer to come." Again, I could relate to Daniel's wait, and my prayer life intensified, as I lay prostrate before the Lord.

During this ordeal, the holidays arrived. At first, we rejected any ideas of having a special Thanksgiving meal. However, we soon realized that we had much to be thankful for and a home to share with others. On Thanksgiving Day we had twenty people around our table. The older girls made homemade pies while others pitched in to fix the turkey and the traditional dishes. I was given permission to sit in a chair at the table as long as my face was resting in the cradle, which looked like a catcher's mitt. Joining us around our table were four families, each with a tale of their own. A drunk driver had killed my adopted sister's parents when she was a child; one family was in transition, moving from one state to another; the other couple was retired; and finally there was our family. I observed, "We have the orphan, the homeless, the elderly, and the blind all giving thanks today." It was a memorable Thanksgiving as we pondered the goodness and loving kindness of the Lord, in spite of everyone's circumstances. We still had life and each other.

Before prayer, I led everyone in singing, "Give thanks with a grateful heart, give thanks to the Holy One, give thanks because He's given Jesus Christ, God's Son. And now let the weak say I am strong, let the poor say I am rich, because of what the Lord has done for us...give thanks."

In twenty-one days, I finally was allowed to raise my head. No wonder Psalm one says, "Blessed is the man who walks with the upright." My hopes were high. The very day that my head was permitted to be erect, my daughters and I were in concert. I had to be assisted onto the stage, but I sang my heart out. Nothing had changed in my passion to serve Jesus Christ. My eyes were patched and I wore dark glasses, but I still had breath to proclaim His love and goodness. I had a holy determination to use all of my losses for His gain.

Despite my hope, the surgery and two others were a disappointment. I had actually been catapulted into more loss of eyesight. As I sat in the examining chair listening to my surgeon explain my condition, the tears fell once again. The eye charts hung in vain as I imagined what it would be like to see perfectly.

Instead, when the doctor summarized his work and my future, he proclaimed, "There is no hope of your ever seeing again." I replied, "No, doctor, you're wrong. There is always hope." He wished us good luck, and our visit was over.

I had again faced a physician who had conveniently summed up my life and stamped on my charts, "No hope." I was outraged to think anyone could ever try to take one's hope. "The arrogance of seeing only what you alone could offer me, doctor, is short-sighted at best," I thought. "It may appear that I am losing this battle with my eyes, but I will not give up hope." It was my only lifeline now in a raging storm.

I had some eyesight left after the dark glasses and patches were removed, but there was no real change.

CHAPTER TWENTY-THREE
SEEING BEYOND FRIENDSHIP

Before I had time to decide how to carve out a place for our son in our sorority house, God gave us a spacious dwelling that had been vacant for nine months and was ready for new life. Our realtor said that the sprawling house had not sold because it was too big and it would take a large, unique family to be interested in it. "Look no further," I thought. The house was a miracle. We sold our other house to a cash buyer and purchased this new homestead for $65,000 less than the asking price, ten days after Connor's birth. We were, indeed, that large, unique family; and God favored us with a steal of a deal. I was seeing a pattern—before Lydia's birth we were given a van, and now a miracle house was provided close to the day of Connor's birth.

Our house was 5,500 square feet on two acres of groomed land, surrounded by twenty-eight mighty oak trees. It was its own private country club with a large in-ground pool, fenced-in tennis court, volleyball and basketball courts, and terraces. God used our "Oaks at Fairview" for many memories and restful days. We hosted gatherings of every kind, including retreats, leadership meetings, parties, and even one graduation. I had a fully stocked party room with supplies for any occasion. One of the most common things said about our events was that you might come to the McWilliams not knowing anyone, but you would leave with newfound friends.

From the first moment we acquired the property, we freely gave it to the Lord. The joy of being able to bless others with our new gift was very satisfying. The most pleasure I had was thinking of new and fun ways to celebrate life and friends. Besides, a house with three commercial refrigerators demanded hospitality.

Our first outdoor dinner party celebrated life. We invited households of all kinds, and we had room for families who had been blessed with even more children than we had.

Some weekend church retreats were held in our home with times of intimate sharing and prayer mixed with laughter and encouragement. Church Christmas banquets, planning sessions, youth-group meetings, and spontaneous gatherings were the norm. I loved any reason to throw a party.

Each summer our girls hosted a sister's pool party. Sisters from many families would intermingle with other girls from elementary to high school age, with no one left out. The memory of it all makes me smile even as I write.

One of my favorite get-togethers was for mothers—a Mom's Night Out each fall. Mothers came in droves. At the last one, sixty-five women arrived for a 6:00 p.m. potluck and left refreshed, some not until 3:00 in the morning. Tony and our children, who were tucked away and not invited to join the fun, said they had never heard such laughter and talking. Obviously, these mommas needed some time away.

One time, Tony and I decided to host a pastor's brunch for many of our colleagues. We wanted to give an event that we wished someone had invited us to attend when we were pastoring. This was the hardest group of all, because twelve pastors and their wives from different church backgrounds came but were guarded and afraid to be vulnerable. When we invited them, we had made it clear that there was no hidden agenda or planned program. We just wanted to honor them for serving the Lord in our city. I had never seen a group struggle more to receive an act of kindness.

Our most frequent events were just parties that I would plan around a variety of themes. There was always some occasion to have people over. When any of my friends turned forty, we would have a celebration to crown her queen. This idea was based on a birthday card I once received that said, "You can decide either to be over the hill or queen of the hill." The tradition began, and turning forty attained a level of royal distinction. One friend had the dubious good fortune of reaching fifty before anyone else in our circle, and we crowned her the "Queen Mum." Whether it was a small intimate visit of a few or a very large party, it didn't matter; our house could accommodate either very easily. There was always room to add more to the fun and fellowship.

Our largest event by far was for our first-born daughter, Anna. She was graduating from high school after being home-schooled for most of her life. I had a vision of not only celebrating her graduation but also her miracle life. Eighteen years previously, she had been shown mercy when the doctors had said there was no hope. Our daughter was now the embodiment of the verse we had stated over her years earlier in her weakened condition. "Anna, you will live and not die and declare what God has done forever." The graduation gala declared to all His goodness and mercy.

For many weeks we planned and prepared the outdoor ceremony and the sit-down dinner for two hundred people at the Oaks at Fairview. We set up our sound system and rented a stage with attached floodlights from the Civic Center. Chairs were set up under the cover of oak tree branches, similar to a wedding with a center aisle.

As the unseasonably cool breeze swept over the outdoor arena and the sun began to search for its horizon, people started to arrive.

We had mowed a neighbor's large empty lot and marked it with balloons and signs for our valet parking. Coming from each corner of the property, families walked together to find their seats. All ages from newborn to eighty-five attended this celebration of life. Everyone sat together as one large family.

Anna, robed in her cap and gown, walked among the trees and through the crowd to the song "Butterfly Kisses." The Lord seemed to personally escort her. Shortly afterwards, the congregation under nature's canopy began to worship as they sang, "Great Is Thy Faithfulness." Throughout the night, different speakers commissioned Anna at her new threshold of life. Special friends from Pennsylvania flew in to surprise her, while others drove from surrounding states in the Midwest. Our family sang and Anna's father and both grandfathers spoke the blessing over her. Afterward, the guests were served dinner on the terrace. We had transformed our tennis court into our reception hall, with tables decorated in purple and gold for our regal guests. That night we truly entered His courts with thanksgiving. From its conception, I had wanted the celebration to encourage other families to embrace His ways. God came to celebrate with us, and many lives were profoundly touched.

During the years, strangers, as well as friends, came to our home. One Sunday when we ministered at a church, I spoke with two people from Georgia who were co-workers on a temporary work assignment in our city. They loved the Lord and, like us, were visitors at the church that night. For some reason, I felt compelled to invite them to dinner and, without hesitation, they accepted my offer.

I could not remember when I had ever asked total strangers who were just passing through town to come for dinner. I was reminded, though, of an instance in the Bible when the children of Israel were admonished to be kind to strangers for they knew what it was like to be sojourners in a foreign land. Then there was another more exciting and intriguing thought that I shared with my girls—the scripture in Hebrews that speaks of "entertaining angels unaware." Since we were not really sure who our strangers were, we decided to serve them like royalty.

The girls helped me set the formal dining room table with our finest china. The kitchen smelled inviting as we prepared a full-course dinner for our mystery guests. The evening was filled with conversation as we learned about our new friends and heard the stories of their coming to Christ. Knowing Him had tenderized all of our hearts, and we shared and laughed for hours.

Later, I signaled the girls to help me in the kitchen as I prepared to serve the dessert. One of my daughters closed the swinging door between the dining room and kitchen so we could talk privately. They all whispered, "Well, are they angels or not?" I smiled, shrugged my shoulders and said, "We may never know." No other guests have ever been watched more closely. After dinner, we all played volleyball, continued to talk, and we sang to them. Before they left, our family spoke the blessing from Numbers 6, "May the Lord bless you and keep you and make His face to shine upon you and be gracious unto you. May the Lord lift up his countenance upon you and give you peace." As we all hugged goodbye, it was evident that strangers had come but friends were leaving.

One unusual luncheon that I hosted was for six of my dear friends. I loved this particular group of ladies because of their diversity. We all worshipped at different congregations, but our common bond was Jesus Christ. The group consisted of a college English professor, a lawyer, a university choral director, a nurse, a psychologist's wife, and a pastor's wife.

I had sent them a special invitation to attend a "Blind Date" luncheon. Because I had recently recovered from a year of eye surgeries, I thought it would be insightful to my friends to demonstrate where I now walked. In a tangible way, they stepped into my shoes for one meal.

One particular guest surprised all of us by coming dressed in a nun's full attire. Perplexed and laughing, I asked her what she was doing. She told us that she had promised herself that she would become a nun first before ever again going out on a blind date. We all laughed hysterically before the lights grew dim for my friends.

After everyone had arrived, my luncheon guests were blindfolded. I probably enjoyed that moment more than the rest. My daughters served us, and they stayed busy since we all needed assistance to take our places in the formal dining room where the table was set with special china and goblets. No party duties had been more entertaining for my daughters than serving this luncheon. Some of my visitors ate with their hands and others were hesitant to make any move. I had to teach them quickly that, even when you are blind, you must use your manners. The noise of forks hitting empty spots on the plates made me laugh as they all concentrated on finding food. Finally, my guests were adapting to their new challenges; however, I noticed something strange. When the blinded ladies would converse, I could hear that they had their heads down. I asked the friend next to me, "Why aren't you lifting your head?" She and the others had postured themselves to let their new burden affect where they looked instead of lifting their heads in the midst of adversity. They commented how I made it look as if I could see normally, and they soon realized that I chose to see. It was apparent that it was only His mercy and grace that helped me make a trial look manageable.

After dessert, my special guests requested permission to take their blindfolds off. Everyone sighed with relief as their eyes adjusted to the light. Soon, the sighs changed to growing laughter as we looked around the table. Our nun imposter complained of a sudden headache, quickly removed her head covering, and rubbed the dents it had left in her forehead. A few should have worn bibs along with their blindfolds because food had spilled down the front of them. We began to laugh harder when one of my honored guests discovered that she had some of the chocolate dessert under her fingernails. If the psychologist's wife could have brought her husband to observe our group encounter, his eyes would have been opened, I am sure.

A strange phenomenon happened simultaneously. After the sighs, laughter, and relief of being able to see again, several at the table began to cry as we suddenly sat in silence. The path we had journeyed now separated as they realized I could not take off my blindfold. Our friendship reached a deeper level of love due to their gallant willingness to understand my loss. I loved them all for that one tender moment. We sat quietly as tears burned my cheeks and I buried my face in my napkin. The God of comfort and mercy would have to lead me from here.

CHAPTER TWENTY-FOUR
SEEING BEYOND
MERCY

Not every day was a reason for a party. Our family also enjoyed the freedom to spread out and find a private space. Our little ones had bedrooms near Tony and me on the first floor, and the older girls occupied the upstairs.

Our yard offered more than the nearby playground, but Lydia and Connor were too young to appreciate the benefits of having their own personal park. However, I found it extremely helpful, as I used the tennis court with its gated fence as a large playpen. They would ride bikes, have fun with their outside toys, run, and play ball as I sat within the court on a park bench, feeling safe. I could not imagine being in an unrestrained, open area, having to watch them with my impaired eyesight. It was always debatable as to exactly who was watching whom. God, in His mercy, was faithfully watching over all of us, and this became very evident one particular spring.

One afternoon, Tony was working in his office on the far east side of the house, and Lydia was playing in her bedroom. Suddenly, without any apparent reason, Lydia stopped playing with her toys and, passing her working father, quickly walked outside. She left through the office door onto the side terrace and, in seconds, opened the large, black, ornate iron gate. The gate, three times her size, did not slow down the stride of this little four-year-old. She was on a rescue mission that no one could see until later. Her path led to the back terrace around the pool, as well as to the lower terrace by the tennis court. As she rounded the corner, she saw only the top of Connor's head in the pool. The pool water was dirty since it was just beginning to turn spring. Moments earlier, Connor had bent over to touch some oak leaves that were floating in the water and, having reached too far, slipped in without anyone knowing he was even outside. Lydia began to scream for help as she ran towards the pool. She demonstrated wisdom beyond her years as she lay prostrate with her stomach on the concrete pool deck and reached out to grab for her brother's hand, pulling him to the side of the pool. Tony had heard her screams and ran just in time to assist lifting two-year-old Connor to safety. Without any doubt, God used Lydia to save Connor's life that afternoon.

Days later, our city experienced some horrific thunderstorms. It was a Monday night and all of our family was home enjoying a quiet evening, except for Lindey who was at the university taking a dance class. Tony and Anna were working in our large office that was surrounded with windows overlooking the property. Lydia and Connor were playing house with their toys in the dining room, where they didn't usually play. Holly was in the laundry room at the back of the house, and I, for one of the first times, had gone to bed early because I was exhausted and felt chilled. God, in His mercy, had carefully positioned each of us for the storm that would rock our world.

A bolt of lightning made a direct strike on a large oak tree by the corner of the windowed office and our master suite. The sound was like that of a bomb exploding over and over as the lightning literally fried the tree. The wet bark on the outside shell and the dry bark within made a natural explosive that nearly was fatal. When the tree was struck, it shot a nine-foot log that literally flew like a deadly missile through the bay window of the master suite. It came into the area where the little ones normally played. God had placed them in one of the safest areas in the house, away from any damage. The other room that was secure was the laundry room where Holly was at the time. I was the closest to the log missile, only about six feet away, but covered up and protected from all the shattered glass that flew in all directions.

A small but damaging piece of the tree penetrated the shingles and lodged into the ceiling in the office. Frightened by the unexpected explosion, Anna immediately fell to her knees, thinking that terrorists had bombed us. Miraculously, none of the glass in the office was even cracked. Another small piece of wood from the exploding tree jumped over a section of the house to our expansive formal living room with three large bay windows. One nine feet bay window was shattered, and the flying glass embedded itself into the carpet and furniture. Amazingly, the bay window nearest the piano was unharmed.

In those horrifying moments, I kept shouting the name of Jesus, as I feared for my family's lives. I could hear Tony searching to find everyone and then shouting, "Run from the house. I smell smoke." Terrified, but without hesitation, we all ran. I was barefoot as I ran through shattered, slivered glass, yet I was not cut anywhere. Without delay, we gathered on the porch and all of us were safe. God had protected us in the middle of the storm, keeping us secure and unharmed.

Neighbors looked on from their porches, trying to find the reason for the explosion. Two couples close to us came to help, and we watched, still in shock, as they stapled tarps over the windows and picked up glass throughout the house. They were amazed, along with us, at the merciful protection of the Lord.

Over the next six months, our house received a facelift: a new roof, new carpeting, new furnishings, and fresh paint. We were terribly inconvenienced by the storm damage, yet so very grateful for His hand of deliverance.

Several weeks later, God used Lydia, once again, to save a life—mine. Lydia's room was not far from our master suite. She had gone to bed in little sleeper pajamas with the feet attached to them and had become uncomfortably hot and restless. In the middle of the night, she came to get in bed with us, but her restlessness awakened her daddy. When Tony became alert, he realized that my breathing was not right. I was slipping into a coma as a result of a dangerously low blood sugar level. Tony hurriedly poured Coke into my mouth and called 911. Later, I learned that I had aggressively fought him with every attempt he made to help me.

When I started to gain consciousness, I was sitting on the side of the bed with Coke covering the front of me. At the same moment, the firemen and rescue squad came bolting through our front door, and the sound of marching boots sounded throughout the house as they paraded to our bedroom suite. Tony gently explained, "Gail, I've called some people to help us." Immediately, I was conscious and said, "Oh no. Does the house look okay for company?"

I remembered nothing. The look of fright lingered on my husband's face, telling all that I had missed. Days earlier, I had been put on a new, synthetic insulin that was harmful to me and proved nearly fatal. God again, in His mercy, used our little one to save my life that Saturday night. Lydia, the very one I had laid down my life to give birth to, had now used her life to save mine.

Though it was around 4:00 a.m. when the fireman left our home and our night had been very traumatic, it did not matter. Early Sunday morning, we still gladly went to church and testified of His mercy. We had walked through the shadow of a death valley one spring, unharmed and safe. Looking back, I wonder why in that one season three attempts by the angel of death had come to raid our home of precious life. I could not help but also wonder what was next for this McFamily.

CHAPTER TWENTY-FIVE
SEEING BEYOND TRANSITION

None of us could have anticipated what came next for our family. We were invited to Texas. Our assignment was to minister as a family at the campus church of a well-known Bible school. Conveniently, we were present during the school's Campus Days, and our two oldest daughters participated in the recruitment activities. Anna loved the school. I had always told my firstborn, "When you leave home, I'm going with you." And so we did. This weekend ministry engagement ended up lasting six years.

This was a divine appointment. After only three short days, everyone in our family knew that we would return. We all had a longing to follow God and move to the Southwest.

We arrived home in Illinois at dawn. Because it was pickup day for the neighborhood garbage, Tony set out the trash cans. Then he deliberately returned to the garage, rummaged through items in the corner, and began immediately to pile junk at the curb. This was our first step toward moving. We knew that "faith without works is dead," and we knew we must ready ourselves for the change we believed was taking place.

I had given explicit instructions on the way home from Texas to keep our proposed move a secret while we prayed more about our radical transition. Everyone agreed. The next day, our little Lydia returned to kindergarten; however, in all the excitement she left her discretion at home. After her absence, she was greeted by the principal, her teacher, and the church secretary, all asking her about the trip. In a loud, excited voice, she said, "We're moving to Texas." The news spread and our phone rang nonstop with curious inquirers for one week. My jaws hurt and sores developed on my tongue from talking on the phone so much, telling and retelling how the Lord was working in our hearts. After twenty-two years, we were leaving our Midwest homeland.

In only a few days, the Bible school offered Tony an administrative position. Our oldest daughter, Anna, enrolled as a student and accepted a part-time job in the Admissions Department. Lindey was asked to be on the dance team, and she and Holly volunteered to work at the six-week summer youth camp. All of us were excited, and we knew we had heard from God.

In two short months we were on our way to a new adventure. I wondered how Abraham of the Old Testament packed up his family, herdsman, livestock, and all of his belongings to move to a city he "knew not of" in obedience to God's leading. We managed to pack everything we needed in a large U-Haul truck and one cargo trailer pulled by our overloaded van—with no livestock, thankfully. Each driver had a walky-talky to use along the journey. Two hours into the trip, we approached the edge of the mighty Mississippi River. As we crossed from Illinois into Missouri, Tony radioed his tribe that followed, "We are getting ready to cross over our Jordan." I radioed back, "Lead on, Moses. Lead on." We excitedly looked forward to a land filled with promise.

God's provision for the trip was sufficient, and our trust was fully in the One who had called our family to go. Three weeks before our departure date, we had ministered at a church in the St. Louis area. They had given us the largest honorarium that we had ever received. It was the full amount that we needed to relocate.

We planned to live temporarily on the campus of this school nestled in the heart of the inner city. Students from sixty-five nations studied here. I was convinced that anyone who lived on this multi-cultural, inner-city campus, sandwiched between two major interstates, was surely being equipped to live anywhere in the world. We arrived at this hub of ministry in the middle of the night. Our caravan had successfully made the journey. The trip was uneventful until the exit to the campus suddenly appeared, and we were in the farthest lane from it. Abruptly, our Moses crossed six lanes of interstate at high speed, exited with a wild ride down the steep ramp, and abruptly stopped at a sudden red light. The rest of the family was right on his bumper with a cargo trailer whipping around behind. Within minutes, we pulled into the campus parking lot. Tony, sounding shaken, asked, "Is everyone all right back there?" He broke our stunned silence by saying, "Welcome to Dallas everyone."

The late-night security guard gave us the key to our "temporary" campus housing. Our thrilling entrance onto campus from the highway had pumped enough adrenalin into us for everyone to unload the cargo trailer that same night. No one had alerted us that the surrounding urban neighborhood was also awake late at night, looking for some action. In our naiveté, we might have put these predators to work, if they had greeted us, while we carried boxes to our new residence that night in May.

We had exchanged our 5,500-square-foot house with two acres for a 1,000-square-foot campus apartment with signs that said to stay off the grass. Not everything in our cargo trailer and the U-Haul truck would fit in our small dwelling. We had to keep most in storage until we could find our Texas house. I quickly calculated that each person had approximately 143 square feet of space; of course, it had to be shared with the furniture. I mused that it is in the small places of life that we realize how much character we really have—or don't have.

During the next few days, we experienced culture shock. One day the girls comforted me by saying, "Mom, we think it is best that you can't see." At one time, the Bible school had been surrounded by an attractive suburb, and prime property among rolling hills and trees. During the years, shifting neighborhoods periodically troubled by crime, drugs, alcohol, and gangs encircled the area. Our apartment complex was once HUD housing that the Bible school had bought and renovated. A tall iron fence created a thin boundary between the adjoining neighborhood and us.

Since I lost my eyesight, I've depended primarily on sound. In our new location, I was over-stimulated. The highway noise was constant background sound that accompanied people living on top of each other in apartment dwellings. At first, I thought the backfiring sounds were from muffler problems. No one told me there were guns in the city. Our windows of thin glass rumbled in the night when helicopters flew low, barely above the treetops. Their searchlights looked like roving disco balls in the sky, searching for people who ought to be in bed. Are these the gated communities that people were raving about in Dallas? We had a gate, but I was not convinced it was for prestige. We knew for certain that we had stepped into a different world when we saw the cardboard sign in front of a store that read, "rent a tire." We were also astonished that people could order chicken and pay their phone bill at the same drive-through. Life had taken on a new dimension for the McFamily.

In spite of the surrounding community, something of great value was happening on the campus. Students were being trained to be world-changers with a passion for the people of the nations. They had proven themselves for over three decades, having been trained to be influential men and women who were salt and light in their generation. Many had been trained for ministry that found its expression in pastoring, missionary work, worship, market place opportunities, key governmental offices, and much more. No matter what changes we faced, we knew our move was strategic. We felt honored to be positioned among them all.

This chapter in our lives had already been described in a classic piece of literature—"It was the best of times, it was the worst of times." On one hand, we had the privilege to search for treasures that most of the world had yet to hear about. Among them were the rich deposit of scriptures, mission trips around the world, weekly guest speakers, internships, and synergy from people who led with vision and tenacity. I challenged my college-aged daughters to look for the buried treasures that would not be lying on the surface. They would have to dig for them. I also encouraged them to make friendships that would last for a lifetime and not just a season. They would learn from some of the finest Christian leaders in the world.

On the other hand, we had been stripped of everything, it seemed. Tony and I had never lived in an apartment, so I wondered why we thought it would be a good idea now, with five children. What was to be a "temporary" housing arrangement on campus lasted five years and four months. God positioned us in the middle of constant activity. There was no rest. Our privacy was limited, and we longed for our own spacious house. Our van's air conditioning failed, and the summer heat was awful. No one knew about the ministry we had established in the Midwest, and no one knew us. We had to rebuild. We had been poured from one small vessel into a larger vessel, and the free fall was unnerving at times.

After nine weeks, Holly answered the phone one afternoon when I was away. She gave me the message that a radio station had called, saying that we had won something. I imagined it would be passes to a water park, since it was the peak of summer, or tickets to a concert. I was shocked when I called them back and heard their declaration. "Your family has been selected as one of the top ten new Christian vocalists in the metroplex." "How do you even know us?" I wondered. Earlier that same year we had released our first family music CD. We later learned that a friend had entered our CD in a citywide contest sponsored by a local Christian radio station. The winners were featured in a large concert at the Will Rogers Coliseum in Fort Worth. That same weekend, on a Sunday afternoon in front of the library in downtown Dallas, thieves broke into our van. Thousands of dollars of sound equipment, recordings of vocal tracks, and irreplaceable original background music were stolen. I wondered how we could win and lose musically all in the same weekend.

Our family was very visible on campus as we spread out to find treasures. In addition to Tony's administrative position, he was called on to teach. We were asked to sing often, and the cofounder of the school was one of our biggest fans. We made friends of every age and from many nations. We opened our small apartment as a hospitality center to students, staff, and alumni. The holidays always created new opportunities to invite students and internationals who had nowhere to go. One Thanksgiving, we prepared two turkeys with all the fixings for almost fifty students.

Later in our extended stay, we were allowed to open the empty neighboring apartment by tearing down the adjoining wall. This added one more bathroom and bedroom and provided 800 more glorious square feet. Before this time, we kept thinking that we would be moving soon. Instead, we realized that God had placed us here in the middle of campus life because He wanted us to open our doors to others. So we set out to make our apartment a home. On our third Christmas, my brother sent us a generous Christmas gift of cash to refurbish our inner city residence. We purchased carpet, lighting, ceiling fans, wallpaper, and paint. Our urban makeover made it feel more like a home.

During the remodeling, the school's maintenance crew worked in our apartment for nearly two months. As an act of appreciation, I invited the entire team for lunch. We had created a banquet table with two eight-foot tables, and people were sitting and standing everywhere. As each worker shared the story about how he or she had come to the Bible school, I realized that twelve nations sat at our table. In that moment, I became aware of how very wealthy we were. No sum of money could purchase what we had found on the campus of Christ For The Nations.

During the last autumn of living on campus, I spoke at a women's rally at a church with a very large, multi-cultural congregation that modeled unity to the world. In the audience was a friend of mine. The two of us had been together several months earlier at a leadership prayer meeting for women in ministry. After that meeting, she had asked if she could drive me home. I respectfully declined her offer, simply because we lived on opposite sides of Dallas. She lived in a prominent part of the city on the north side, and I lived on the south side. However, she insisted. I finally agreed, for I, too, wanted to spend time with her. On the ride home, I remarked, "Wow. Look how much society has changed. You, my friend, are the African American living in "yuppyville," and driving your Land Rover to take this white woman home to the ghetto." We laughed, as did my friend's sister, who accompanied us. When we arrived at our campus apartment, my friend walked me to my door. Later, she told that her sister had been frightened while waiting in the vehicle, even though it was daylight, and she hurriedly had locked all the car doors.

When I shared this with the women at the rally, there was a roar of laughter. Boldly and with unexpected gratitude, I declared, "It has been good for this white woman to have lived in the ghetto for five years." Immediately, the women began to applaud with fervor. It was at that moment that I recognized how much God had enriched my life through all the difficult changes involved with our move. My experiences had helped me win the respect and love of my audiences.

The "best of times and the worst of times" had woven golden threads throughout the brilliant and colorful tapestry God was making of our lives. Such rich fabric could not be humanly manufactured.

Our living situation was not the only thing that had changed since we came to Texas—my heart had, too.

CHAPTER TWENTY-SIX
SEEING BEYOND DANGER

After coming to Dallas, fatigue was a constant challenge for me, and rightly so, I thought. Who wouldn't be exhausted after the life changes and the move we had made?

However, after several months, I was alarmed at the severity of my fatigue. I remarked that I was not handling the heat of the southwest summer very well. I would ask Tony to take my purse the short distance from our parking space to our front door because carrying it added to my exhaustion. Walking into the cool apartment was a relief, but I didn't feel refreshed. It seemed strange to be so worn out simply by walking down the twelve-foot hallway to our bedroom. Perhaps I needed a vacation with some extra iron pills. Only my family knew of my weariness though, because I just kept going.

Later in the summer when we performed as winners of the radio talent search, I asked for a chair as I waited backstage for the master of ceremonies to introduce us. When he called our names, I gained a new energy to walk across the stage to sing with the girls. God had graced me with the help I needed; however, I did not understand my problem.

One day, Tony called a physician friend and asked for his help. The first thing Ron did was check my pulse. Alarmingly, it was only in the thirties. "No wonder you're tired, Gail!" He wanted me to go immediately to the hospital, but I thought a few nights of good sleep would help me.

In a matter of days, Ron again made a house call and checked my pulse. This time it was in the twenties, and I could barely lift my head off the couch to even acknowledge his visit. He convinced me that this was serious, and that I must go to a cardiologist. I was too tired to fight, so I agreed.

I called the doctor Ron had referred me to, and I was in the cardiologist's office within hours. I sat quietly on the end of the examining table and stared at the wall while Tony stood behind me with the cardiologist, studying the results of the EKG alongside him. "I know exactly what it is. She needs a pacemaker!" I turned my head suddenly to look at the two men conferring about my condition. "A pacemaker? I'm still a young woman!"

He said that my heart's electrical system had snapped, and the lower part of my heart was not engaged with the top part. He excused himself from the room as Tony and I sat in silence.

When the doctor stepped back into the room, he handed Tony a brochure about my condition and then said he had reserved a room at Baylor hospital for that day. "Wait! This is moving too fast. I haven't even prepared my children, let alone myself!" Reluctantly agreeing to let me delay one day, he recommended another doctor because he was leaving the next morning on vacation.

Just thinking about changing doctors again added more stress. After the appointment, I stood on the curb of the medical clinic waiting for my husband to bring the van. Tears fell as I wondered if the reason we had been brought to Dallas was to connect with superb medical care.

My exhaustion had actually started six months before we had moved when Anna, Lindey, Holly and I had recorded our first CD. This project involved many late nights, too much caffeine, and continual stress. Looking back, I remembered the exact night and the specific song we were taping when I suddenly felt a weariness that I had never known. We were recording "On Eagle's Wings," and were struggling with the final chorus. For some reason, we could not reach the standard of excellence that we wanted. It was midnight, and we had been recording for hours.

At the same time, our temperamental engineer began to have his own breakdown, of sorts. He did not share our faith and, in fact, embraced black magic. I knew that this had been part of our battle on many occasions. Though we were minutes from finishing, he angrily announced, "I need a smoke break. What are you doing? Trying to kill me?"

I looked at the girls and signaled them to pray. Disturbed by his lack of professionalism and his sudden outrage, I suggested that we continue another day. He yelled, "Just take a break for one hour and then return to the studio." I agreed, with no fight left in me.

The girls and I sat in a restaurant for an hour. I could hardly walk, and I asked Anna to assist with my things. Fortunately, we finished the project that night without any more drama.

Shortly after the CD was released, we traveled through several states to promote our new musical effort. It was during these days of touring that we first came to Texas as guests of Christ For The Nations. God, in His mercy, had moved me to a place where doctors make house calls. At Ron's persistence, I had finally found the reason for the fatigue and its solution.

Just as I settled in under the covers, wondering what the next day would bring, the phone rang. The call was from a doctor I didn't know. It was 11:00 p.m. After identifying himself, he asked, "Gail, where are you?" I thought his was a strange question because he had just called me at my home. "I've been all over the hospital trying to find you. You were referred to me concerning your heart condition."

Surprised, I asked, "How serious is this?" He replied, "Gail, you are in total heart block!"

After a short conversation, the new cardiologist said that he would see me in his office first thing in the morning. He consoled himself and me by saying, "Well, you've stayed alive this long, so I trust you'll be fine until the morning."

The following day I was suited with a heart monitor until the doctors could determine what action they wanted to pursue. I was relieved to have four days before they needed me back at the doctor's office, because I was scheduled to be a hostess at a women's conference.

I just kept going. I hoped for a miracle so I could cancel my appointment with the surgeon. Instead, I continued to feel exhausted.

On the second day of the conference, I needed a ride to the campus auditorium. Tony was using our only vehicle, so Anna called to say that she would be over to pick me up. She arrived, asking if I was ready for an adventure. She had come with a campus golf cart. We laughed then, but now I shudder to think that I was wired to a heart monitor while out for an inner city cruise in a golf cart with my new chauffeur.

One week after the initial heart diagnosis, doctors placed a pacemaker in my body. Immediately, I had a pulse of eighty and felt great. I asked the doctor if I was considered bionic, with my newly inserted machine. I felt like it.

God had preserved my life again. Though many can quote the twenty-third Psalm, "Though I walk through the valley of the shadow of death, I will fear no evil for you are with me," few want to test that verse. I had not realized how close to death I had been walking, but everyone recognized that God was obviously with me.

Over the years, I had been accustomed to walking alongside danger with His grace keeping me safe. When my children faced danger, however, I didn't handle it well at all.

It was three days before Christmas, but our apartment had no Christmas decorations. Our tradition for the holidays was to set up a borrowed tree and dream we were somewhere else, vacationing. However, this particular year, our dream had come true. We were all packing and gathering borrowed winter coats and scarves in preparation for skiing. My brother's family was hosting a Big Sky, Montana, Christmas. Everyone on my side of the family was planning to be there, and we couldn't wait. We had decided that flying to the mountains on Christmas Eve would be our family gift.

On Monday evening before we left, everyone had some kind of errand to run. The older girls were working overtime at their jobs, and Tony had just wrapped up his office responsibilities.

I was going to the mall with Tony and the two youngest children to find Lydia some boots. From there, Tony was going to take Connor with him, and Holly was coming afterward to pick up Lydia and me at the mall. A rush of last minute shoppers filled the store as we stood in the shoe department. Just moments before Tony and Connor were about to leave us, my cell phone rang. It was Holly.

"Mom, I don't think I am going to be able to pick you up at the mall tonight." I leaned up against the shoe display listening and trying to figure out an alternate plan for all the errands at hand. "Holly, why can't you come?" Her voice changed, and I could tell she was crying, which was unusual for my tower of strength. "Mom, a gunman entered our apartment and I've been robbed." "Holly, are you okay? Did he touch you?" She told me she was safe at the neighbor's apartment, waiting for the police.

I was so thankful that Tony and Connor had not already left us. Speeding home, we drove up to the apartment complex just as the police arrived. Together, we heard what had happened as a composed Holly told the police her story.

Earlier that evening, the trespasser apparently had been watching our apartment and saw us leave. Lindey left soon after we did. Holly was sitting across the room when the front door opened. She thought that Lindey had forgotten something and had returned for it. However, when she stood up and turned around, she looked into the face of an intruder who carried a shotgun. He abruptly ripped the phone out of the wall and asked Holly for her cell phone. Holly told him that she had just given it to her sister. He then demanded money. Thankfully, Holly had $116 in a large stack of one-dollar bills in her billfold. She had worked as a valet parking attendant that day and had earned the money from tips. As the man reached for the money, Holly pulled it from her wallet, using her finger to push down her debit card; then she wisely threw the wallet to the corner of the room. As he grabbed the cash, the thief warned her that his buddies were just outside the window watching her every move, and he ordered her to stand still after he left. He threatened her by saying that he knew where she lived, and he would be back.

As quickly as he had come, he left, leaving the door open behind him. Holly stood perfectly still just as she had been ordered. Within minutes, the gunman returned and stared at her. In his taunting arrogance, he repeated, "Don't think about moving." And again, he disappeared.

Holly remained frozen in place. Finally, she swiftly walked to the door and closed it, undecided as to what her next move should be. She considered going to her car, but feared the man was still nearby. Instead, she ran upstairs to neighbors we barely knew and knocked loudly. As soon as someone opened the door, Holly stepped inside, pulled the door closed behind her and asked to use their phone to call the police and then her mother. She remained remarkably composed until she heard my voice.

As a police officer took her report, he seemed more upset than Holly. He described what might have happened to her and warned that the criminal might return. He even advised us to move immediately. He frightened all of us. The officer did compliment Holly on her strength of character, and he was obviously impressed with how she had responded to a dangerous situation. He told her, "You should consider a career in law enforcement." If Holly did ever pursue that career, we know she would not be as dramatic and talkative as this young man.

Our Montana Christmas was one of our best ever, and helped to dim the memory of the frightening incident. Times of danger and times of joy continued to fill our days in the city. Over and over the Lord gave us glimpses of our destiny beyond any danger. It was evident that He held our lives in His hands, and none of us walked alone. Continually, I heard His promptings to trust and not be afraid. Little did I know that trust would be needed even when I thought I was safe.

CHAPTER TWENTY-SEVEN
SEEING BEYOND
THE OFFENSE

One of the joys of motherhood has been the times I sing with my three older daughters. There is no comparison to a tight, family blend of harmony when it comes to music. When our four voices blend, many have remarked that we have the sound of the Lennon Sisters from decades ago. I taught my daughters how to sing not only simple chords, but also how to make lush harmonies. This is especially delightful when we sing a cappella.

Music always accompanied us on our journey. We have sung before queens as well as at Dairy Queens. Our humorous cow song was played on the radio during Dairy Awareness Month. Even in the most difficult of times and challenges, our family's love for music has enabled us to sing. I sang while pregnant with every baby I carried. I would ask my audience, "How many of you have come expecting to receive of the Lord?" Then, I would turn sideways and help them visualize just what "expecting" might look like. My admonition to them would always be to not let go until God had "delivered" them.

A few days before one Thanksgiving, we were shopping at Sam's Club. The store was packed, and the lines were very long. While the cashier checked us out, I summoned the girls to gather around me to sing a blessing to her while she worked on our order. The girls had learned not to refuse my request to sing because they knew it would be a losing battle. The cashier smiled, thanked us, and then ordered us to wait while she left her post. We stood in obedience, though I was conscious of the long line behind us. Soon, the cashier returned with a small cell phone, or so we thought; in reality it was a microphone. She then demanded, "Sing!" So we did.

The store quieted as people stopped talking. I wondered at the time, "Who gets the opportunity we just had to wish 'Happy Holidays' to the patrons of a busy Sam's?" Upon finishing, we grabbed our cart to leave. When the Sam's manager checked our receipt, I couldn't resist asking, "Who was singing in your store?" She said, "I don't know, but it was beautiful! I wonder who it was?" Smiling, I wished her a great day.

Holidays are perfect for singing spontaneously. One Christmas Eve, friends had taken us to dinner. After eating, we called the waiter over to our table to thank him for his excellent service, and we asked if we could sing to him. Softly, we began, "Have Yourself a Merry Little Christmas" with those lush chords. He smiled as we serenaded him. The longer we sang, the quieter the restaurant grew. Of course, the quieter the restaurant, the louder we became as we seized our new stage for a holiday performance. It wasn't long until the only sounds you could hear in the crowded restaurant were forks on plates and the McWilliams girls singing. At the end of our song, the entire restaurant applauded. I stood to my feet during their applause and lifted my glass of water as though I were toasting each person there. "Let's all sing!" I said, as I led, "We Wish You a Merry Christmas." Everyone joined in, making it a true Hallmark Moment.

We have sung at restaurants, on street corners, in doctor's offices, and at malls. It is not surprising that the youngest McWilliams daughter can sing as well. However, we four seasoned singers always end up being her backup as she takes the front stage.

Connor, too, has a nice voice but always prefers the speaking parts as he inspires his audience by quoting parables from the scriptures. He has followed in his dad's footsteps. I am amazed at the willingness of my children to simply give of themselves. I love hearing my family speak or sing the blessing over someone's life. It takes so little to encourage another and simply say thanks.

Of course, we also were invited to sing for banquets, churches, theaters, television specials, radio programs, and other events. All have been memories I cherish—except for one.

Two weeks before Christmas, the girls and I were asked to be part of a family Christmas presentation for a church that was dear to us. I loved the idea of having households of faith use their talents to celebrate the birth of the King of Kings. The program included skits, readings, and other artistic expressions of worship, along with several families singing.

The director called a dress rehearsal to ensure having the proper lighting and appropriate sound levels on the microphones. Because we had a conflict, she excused us and said that someone would stand in for our family during the rehearsal.

As I stepped into the auditorium on opening night, a friend, whom I had not seen for months, approached me. I was so glad to see her because her name had been given to me for one of my prayer assignments, and I had been wondering about her life. As I greeted her, she said directly, "You'll probably hear this from someone else, so I thought I'd tell you first." With guarded laughter, she confessed, "I pretended to be you last night when I filled in for you at the dress rehearsal. I grabbed some others to be your daughters." I listened as she told how funny it had been and how everyone had laughed as she acted blind. I tried to imagine just what she had imitated.

She was not aware that this news might be difficult for me to hear, and she did not seem to realize that she should apologize for her lack of discretion. I perceived that she had simply come to ease her conscience. Once again, she told me how very funny it had been. As she walked away, I looked for a private place to process this unexpected news, so I asked one of my daughters if she would take me to the restroom. How could the most painful struggle of my life be someone else's comedic relief? Why did she feel the need to tell me about it, since I had missed the impromptu comedy club performance? One of my greatest concerns was that someone in my family would hear this news and be hurt. I wanted to protect them as I wished they could have protected me. Immediately, I knew that I must forgive. However, questions, emotions and unbelief flooded me as I stood in a church designed to help others believe.

I was caught off guard by being mocked because I had always felt the respect of others as they applauded my courage. And yet, I have known more than anyone that it has been His courage and His strength that people have seen. Now, I wondered if the entire world were laughing. Did anyone care enough to stop the comedy skit? Can the church pray for you and mock you with the same heart? No matter what the questions were, I knew that immediate forgiveness was the answer to my pain.

Struggling, I gathered my thoughts and emotions, put on my acting skills, and looked for my daughters. Reading my face, each of them asked if I was all right. Calculating my every move, I assured them that all was well, and God wanted to use us that night.

Everyone involved in the production met in the chapel before the service to hear last-minute instructions and to pray together. When I entered, one of the leaders of the church walked up to me and was laughing as he told me about the comedy routine of the previous night. He told me more information than the guilty party had revealed, saying that my imposter had fallen down the steps while the audience laughed. I stood wondering why he and others felt the need to tell me about something that was inappropriate and so distasteful to me. What was I to do with the information? "Did everyone think it was funny to mock me?" I asked him. After reading my face, he quickly changed the subject.

I wondered how I would make it through the night. I cried inside, "Jesus, help me to forgive."

Before leaving the chapel, I asked my daughters to pray over me. They asked what was wrong, but I just told them that the enemy was trying to trip me up and I needed their help. The walk to the auditorium was the longest of my life. I had lost my footing and I was vulnerable. I had never felt more blind in all of my life.

When it was finally our turn to sing, I took hold of Anna's arm. We both tripped over cords as we groped to find our way to the darkened stage. My confidence was missing.

We had chosen to sing a song that was new for us and the harmony, though beautiful, was extremely difficult. The selection focused on peace in a world of conflict. How I longed for that peace at this very moment.

When we started to sing, we missed our harmony. We had never made a mistake of this magnitude. "We will just try again," I said. We tried once more and still could not find our places. For the first time in my life, I thought we were going to have to sit down and say we just could not sing. No gracious exit or resolution could be found. I knew my daughters were wilting on stage, and yet they persevered. We tried one more time, one by one entering into harmony, as we staggered our notes until we could land the first chord. We only missed the first word of full harmony but it seemed like an unending musical score. At the end of the song, the warm applause by the kind people in the audience, expressing their love and support, poured ointment into our wounds. Oh, the dread of realizing that we had to do it again tomorrow at two more performances. After the program, our family stood on the church sidewalk talking with people. A young man from the youth group, who was a friend of our daughters, came over to say that we were still his favorite singers. I began to joke with him as we all laughed. I called him by name and said, "Well, I guess last night's comedy routine was prophetic after all because we did, indeed, fall off the stage." His laughter stopped and a very pained expression came across his face as he said, "I am so very sorry."

Our family had come to the performance at different times that evening, so we had multiple cars between us. I chose to ride home with my daughter, Holly. I had already decided that I would process my pain in private. However, my thoughts were interrupted when my daughter said through sobs, "After tomorrow, I will never again step back into that church." I thought she was just embarrassed by our slippery start to a beautiful song; however, she went on to say, "Mom, I heard everything."

We couldn't talk the entire way home; we just sobbed together. Proverbs 18:14 best summed up where I was at this moment. "The spirit of a man will sustain his infirmity; but a wounded spirit who can bear?" God's grace had made our suffering look easy to those around us, but they had not seen the tears of desperation and loss as we had cried to find His joy in the midst of our darkest hours.

I sat in the car thinking how much different an encouraging word and a prayer for my obvious loss would have meant to any of us. No one in that church knew that one of the most difficult challenges of my life had been placed in my hands a few weeks earlier. I had picked up a white cane for the first time so I could learn to walk independently. At first, that white cane seemed like a flag of surrender, waving to show everyone that I had lost the battle. However, I had come to grips with the fact that it was simply a tool in my hands to assist me in being even more mobile. My deepest fear was of falling. The greatest concern of my family was helping me not to fall. Was the church world entertained as I struggled to walk through an uninvited misery?

When we entered our apartment, everyone was sitting around the table waiting for us. I quickly walked to the bedroom. However, they had seen my red eyes, as well as Holly's, and thought we had been arguing. As I paced in the bedroom, crying out to God, I decided that I could not bear this burden alone. I joined the family at the table, and Holly and I told our story. All of us sat in stunned silence and tears quietly flowed. A close friend looked on from the kitchen. My indignant husband broke the short-lived silence saying, "This is appalling!" Didn't anyone know the depth of hardship this journey has been? Didn't anyone stand up at the rehearsal to say this is wrong?

I knew we could not be like the climbers I had heard about who had been exploring one of the "safer" glaciers in the north. A tragic accident occurred when one of the climbers fell. Because the climbers were tied together at the waist, they all fell.

I spoke to my family with a strong directive that we must forgive immediately and not have a similar, tragic fall. We couldn't be strapped together for life with this offense. We bowed in prayer and laid our hurting hearts at the feet of the One who also had been mocked and offended by His own people. We wanted to model our response after His example when He cried, "Forgive them, Father, for they don't know what they are doing."

Regardless of whether they meant to hurt us or simply did not think about the consequences, it was immaterial now. We must choose to forgive, and we did. I battled many thoughts after that weekend but found my refuge in the scriptures. As I reflected on the stakes of a resentful heart, Psalm 119:165 came to mind. "Great peace have they who love Thy law, and nothing shall offend them."

I made many attempts to call and email my offender so the matter might be handled according to the scriptural instruction in Matthew 18:15. "Moreover if your brother sins against you, go and tell him his fault between you and him alone. If he hears you, you have gained your brother." Weeks later, she emailed an apology to me. However, the others who participated never showed concern over the deep wound our family had experienced. Only the church leader, who called and wrote immediately to ask forgiveness for his insensitivity, attempted to make amends.

I wondered how many people have lived a life bound by offenses while missing the surprise that waits just beyond forgiveness.

CHAPTER TWENTY-EIGHT
SEEING BEYOND SURPRISE

I love surprises. However, I never could have imagined the surprise that lay just beyond the offense. The holidays were over, and the new year began with an unexpected call from a prominent businessman, saying, "Gail, you've been highly recommended to speak to our company. Would you consider speaking in February to the Ziglar Corporation?" He went on to say, "I would like to schedule it when Zig is in town because I know he will want to meet you."

I was about to experience a shower of surprises from an open heaven. I am confident that this call would not have come if I had held on to unforgiveness. When I released what I was clutching in my hand to God, He was free to release what he was offering in His hand to me. I could not imagine how very big His hand must be.

Eleven months prior, I had told my husband in casual conversation, "Tony, I would like to speak for some corporations this year and have lunch with Zig Ziglar." I desired those two requests because of what they symbolized. Corporate America thrives on vision, and I was confident that the message of hope would work there, too. Mr. Ziglar represented the granddaddy of all motivators. Though I never had the privilege of reading any of his books or seeing him in person, I still knew that he was a world renown, enthusiastic life-coach for multitudes. I admired his uncompromising faith in God and his authentic love for helping others.

Earlier in the fall, I was asked to speak at two large corporations in Dallas. There, my belief in the extent to which people respond to a message of hope was confirmed. My audiences laughed and then cried as I purposely reached for their hearts. It came natural to me to encourage these corporations about greatness as I challenged them to see beyond the day with both vision and hope. The response was more than I could have imagined.

I was scheduled to speak at the Ziglar Corporation the week of February 21. When I saw how unusually full my week was, I exclaimed aloud, "God is taking me to 'launch' this week." I looked forward to what He would show me. My "launch" started with an early Monday morning appointment to speak for the Ziglar Corporation. I was given thirty minutes to direct employees to focus on something, or rather Someone, greater than themselves. Mr. Ziglar sat on the front row taking notes.

At first, I was a bit intimidated and wondered if I was being "launched" out too far. However, my nervousness lasted only a few short minutes because I was on a mission with a message, and I wanted to make the most of my time. At the conclusion of my talk, I took my seat as Mr. Ziglar stood to speak. I wondered at first why he was silent, and then I realized he was crying. He publicly told me that he had never been more impacted by the love of God. He invited me to speak to his large Sunday School class that meets in the chapel of one of the great mega-churches in the Dallas area. He complimented my skills as an effective and articulate communicator and then told me, "You must write your story for the masses to read."

I sat with my heart full of wonder, barely able to receive the kind words of encouragement. It was as though I had passed the inspection of the skilled expert as I sat on the launch pad, and he had instructed me to start my engines. I realized this was a divine appointment.

The next day I spoke at Christ For The Nations. I had been asked to teach at the School of Family and Children's Ministries. There were twelve nations represented among these students—reaching the world had never been easier. When my allotted time ended, the director of the school said that she would alter the morning schedule if I would keep speaking. I was aware of a new level of anointing as I embraced the privilege of encouraging the students. Afterward, the class surrounded me and prayed over me.

Two days later I spoke for the Lions Club in a suburb of Dallas. I thoroughly enjoyed the challenge of bringing a message that was pertinent to a diverse group of people. I greeted the friendly den of Lions by reminding them of Helen Keller who had commissioned the Lion's Club to assist others who could not see. For many years they have provided glasses for underprivileged people. I, too, was interested in helping others to have better vision.

After delivering my message of encouragement, I told them how I personally had found strength to face each new day because of the Lion of Judah and what a difference He had made in my life. As I returned to my seat during their applause, the president touched my arm and whispered that the crowd was standing, an honor he had never seen this group give. I was humbled by the response and thankful for the president's eyes that saw for me the appreciation of my audience. I stood, wanting to applaud the Lord for His goodness and love.

For the next two days, I led a women's retreat for a church from Fort Worth. This is one of my favorite things to do. I like connecting people who may sit together in church but don't know each other. I like modeling transparency to encourage them to be transparent with one another and with God. This group willingly followed my lead, and our hearts were knit together to each other—and to His.

As the week neared its end, I knew that my launch was successful, and I asked the Lord to show me what it all meant. It seemed that He had opened four doors to me. The first with Mr. Ziglar, represented corporate America. The second door, at CFNI, represented the door to the nations. The third door represented the door to the community through the Lions' Club. The final door represented reaching the Church. I told the Lord I was willing to walk through all four doors with His leading.

In the middle of that same week of going to "launch" with God, I received some important phone calls that literally opened the world to me. The afternoon that I returned home from the Lions club, I checked my voice mail. The first message was from Mr. Ziglar himself. He asked if I would call him back and said he hoped that I did not mind his calling a few people about me.

Another call started with, "Hello, Gail, this is the guest coordinator for *Life Today with James and Betty Robison.* Zig Ziglar called us today with a strong recommendation to have you on our program as a guest. We would like to interview you. Could you please call us?" I had to call my husband at work to anchor myself to some kind of rock because I was floating to the ceiling. Within the hour, I had returned Mr. Ziglar's call and been pre-interviewed by phone for an upcoming telecast of the *Life Today* show.

Within four weeks, I taped the television show in front of a live, energetic studio audience with a potential viewing audience of 120 million households around the world. One month later, I spoke to the Christian Legal Society where I stood before lawyers, judges, and a former Texas Supreme Court Justice. I was amazed by His surprises.

I am intrigued when I think about God, who delights in knowing the path of my life and develops my personality to match that destiny. As a child, I can remember preparing for the places that God has now given me. Much to my parents' dismay, I never liked to go to bed. Finally, after a nightly tug of war and my inevitable surrender, I was in my room, sleepy or not. With my door closed and all the lights out, I would stand on the bed and pretend it was my stage. At the age of five, through my vivid imagination, I traveled with Bob Hope as a background singer to entertain and encourage our military troops overseas. When I was fifteen years old, I did have the privilege of singing to the Air Force Academy cadets in their chapel. Amazingly, I still feel at home on a stage, encouraging the "troops."

In my pre-teen years, I used my hairbrush as a makeshift microphone and pretended I was a background vocalist for Anne Murray on the Mike Douglas talk show. In my mind, I was booked every afternoon on some television program.

Early in my high school years, I began to live my dream. While attending school, I traveled part-time with an evangelistic singing team. I had been given the opportunity to exchange my hairbrush for a real microphone. During my young adult years, I sang with a traveling band, a trio, and then debuted as a solo artist. Eventually, I combined singing with speaking. I married a man who was very familiar with the stage, and he loved teaching the truths of the Bible along with new insights at churches and seminars. The spotlight eventually included all our family as our children learned to sing and minister.

Along the way, I have gathered each flower of praise and compliment into a beautiful, fresh bouquet that I willingly give back to the Lord at the end of the day. He, alone, has booked each stage in theaters of His choosing and given the life-message that has affected a variety of audiences. The greatest surprise of all is that He has used my weakness to exemplify how very strong He is.

CHAPTER TWENTY-NINE
SEEING BEYOND THE CHALLENGE

I have never been one to patiently endure other people's excuses. Everyone has some kind of challenge to overcome or to see beyond. The deception is in thinking that your specific trial is by special design and unlike anyone else's. The reality is that trials are common to mankind. The hope for me is based on the scripture that says, "He has made a way of escape." When we pray, He receives our invitation to get involved in our lives and then brings His redeeming power to any challenge.

I credit God for my strong determination in the midst of the challenges of life. His grace has made the road I walk look easier than it often is.

In some situations and on many days, I, too, have been tempted to give up. Then, I ask myself, "Give up to what and to whom?" Soon, I regroup and resolve not to quit. In my black and white world, I realize that I can either sit down or keep dancing. Who wants to be a wallflower, anyway? Life is the challenge, and figuring out how to jump obstacles is the adventure.

At first, it was hard for me to ask for help. At times, it is still frustrating to have to share my journey with others that must come alongside to assist me. It is very humbling not to appear perfect and perhaps to be vulnerable. Still, I contend that it is inner vision that helps you see in the darkest places of life. Trust enables you to take one more step, knowing that you don't have to see the end of the road. Determination is the backbone to stay in the race. Finishing well is the prize.

Some challenges can only be conquered with a vivid imagination and a sense of humor. When I travel by air, I have to submit to a physical search because of my pacemaker. This used to embarrass me because I didn't want to be different from everyone else. Now, I just consider myself privileged to have such personal care. This search provides an opportunity to tell my story to everyone from the attendants to the airport security personnel. Besides, my line is always shorter than the one for those who appear to be "normal." Thinking about it, why would I want to be just like everyone else anyway?

A unique perspective can also change a negative attitude. Doctors' appointments have interrupted my whole life. I always like to ask the doctor how he is before he can ask me, and when the doctors lay hands on me, I am silently praying for them. Recently, I had finished such a doctor's exam and visit. As we both stepped to the receptionists' desks, I cheerfully said, "Ladies, he is looking good. I don't want to see him again for three more months." Everyone, including the doctor, laughed.

Asking for rides is still a pain and very humbling. I dread feeling rejected and disappointed if I am turned down. Also, I hate to inconvenience others. I have tried to work around this challenge but with no success. Living in Dallas has convinced me, based on some of the wild driving escapades here, that even a blind woman could probably get a license. My only solace is to dream of the day when I will drive again. I am confident that I will be the first to say, "Anyone need a ride?" It makes me wonder exactly who will want to be the first one to ride with me.

One summer, a friend offered me a ride. As I arrived at a 4th of July picnic, my friend pulled up on her four-wheeler, saying, "Get on; let's go." So, off we went. It was so much fun. We toured the farm and rode through the fields and down to the pond. To my surprise, she returned to the party barn, got off the four-wheeler, and said, "Your turn to drive." Loving the challenge, I moved to the front as she got on behind me, and off we went again. She would tell me in my ear whether to go straight or which way to turn as I drove slowly. Within minutes, my friend exchanged places with my husband. Little by little, I grew confident as a blind driver and, obviously, my husband was a man of faith to ride with me. Our speed increased as we drove down to the pond and around the trees. I can still hear his instructions: "Turn right. Straighten up. Now, full throttle." I had not known a more liberating moment since losing my eyesight than that day when the wind blew in my face and the open sky invited me to soar like an eagle—and I was in the driver's seat.

After all the fun, my husband said that a crowd had gathered to watch me drive. Among them were our mortician friends whom I accused of looking for new business. Conquering my challenge that day encouraged the watching crowd to enjoy life a little more themselves.

As a public figure, there are always challenges that have nothing to do with blindness. I was asked to sing at the funeral of a friend's elderly mother. The family had requested an old song that I knew, but, in the middle of it, I forgot two of the verses. So, I made them up. And, they were beautiful—so much so that the family and others in the audience later asked me for a copy of the words. However, I had no idea what they were; I was just grateful the song was over.

One of the funniest challenges I had with a speaking engagement came in Ohio. I had been asked to speak for two Saturday sessions for a ladies' celebration and then be the guest speaker for their two Sunday morning services. There can be no greater challenge than to speak four sessions in a row without notes.

Everything went well until the first Sunday morning service. Living as a diabetic with countless shots and blood testing, I have folded into my life and made routine the challenge of this disease. This morning was no different. Because I have been insulin-dependent since I was a child, I normally test my blood sugar at every meal and before bed; however, if I detect any changes in my body, then I test more frequently. Also, before I am to speak, I make sure that my blood is at a safe level. I always carry a small blood testing machine and some insulin in my purse. Usually, there is not a problem, but this Sunday was an exception.

I was sitting with my two oldest daughters who had come to minister with me in song and then I was going to speak. I began to feel as if my blood sugar level was dropping near the time I was going to be introduced. From my calculations, I figured that I had about five to six minutes before it was my turn. This was too close for comfort. Plus, I could not imagine why my blood sugar level would be so low at this time of day. I had always been afraid that this might happen right before I was to speak somewhere.

I pulled out my blood testing machine and discretely took the test. My blood was dangerously low and dropping steadily. I pulled a Sprite from my purse and a bag of M&Ms. My concern was that they would frown on any food in the sanctuary; but, on the other hand, they might frown on the guest speaker passing out on the front pew. I quickly tried to care for myself. Usually, this stash of sugar would be sufficient, but I had caught the count too late. In a panic, I whispered to my daughter, Anna, "Go find me something fast." She immediately left through a side entrance and returned with a carton of juice and a glass. Thankfully, the congregation was still singing, but it was the final verse.

During the song, we were to prepare our hearts for communion that was scheduled next. In this particular church, their custom was to partake of the wafer and cup of juice when it was passed. Lindey was sitting on my left and Anna on my right. Next to Anna was the pastor's wife, who was watching us from the corner of her eye. Lindey took her communion, but her small communion cup was leaking grape juice everywhere. She signaled Anna to get mine for me; I could not reach for one more thing because I had M&Ms in one hand and a glass of orange juice in the other. Anna took two of everything because she was going to hold on to mine until my hands were free. Instead of the usher seeing our dilemma and moving on, he whispered loudly, "You have to take it all now and then put it back." We were well aware of our making a scene on the front pew. The usher was nervous because he was losing his place in formation with the other ushers who were marching down the aisle in synchronized movement, serving each row of church members. Finally, we juggled everything and I received what surely appeared to others to be my "first communion."

The stress of that moment, along with my abnormal blood sugar level, was a challenge. I told Anna to tell the pastor's wife that I didn't think I was going to be all right by the time the introduction was over. She, too, began to fight her own uneasiness on the front row with us. To this day, I am not certain what happened, except that the Lord helped me. In only moments, the pastor began our introduction and then welcomed us to the platform. I gave a thumbs-up to the pastor's wife, and the girls escorted me to the stage. We sang and then they left me standing alone to speak to my waiting audience. Thankfully, the second service was free of any drama.

Sometimes, we focus too long on our inabilities, not seeing beyond them to the One who is able.

CHAPTER THIRTY
SEEING BEYOND TODAY

Vision requires seeing beyond any situation and finding its value, always trusting. If I had chosen my life's path, it would not have included blindness. However, my passion has always been to let the Father use me to advance His kingdom and encourage His people, and He continues to refine me. Rather than offering textbook theology and pat answers, I have chosen to be transparent. Someone once stated, "A mind only reaches a mind, but a life can reach a life." My desire has been to touch as many lives as I possibly can in my lifetime.

I can't imagine that anyone ever lives life thinking that someday his or her story will be told in a book. Yet, the scriptures remind us that everyone around us is reading our lives. I struggled at first to even write this book. I didn't think anyone would be interested, and I didn't want the hard work of writing to be only an exercise in vanity. After all, who is Gail McWilliams anyway?

One day, a friend of mine nailed me to the wall. He, along with others, had been insisting that I sit down and write my story. I responded to his encouragement with my usual excuses. He turned to me and said, "Gail, if you don't think your story is worth writing, then quit telling it." For the first time, I was able to hear the truth. God had given me a story of His triumph and the joy of choosing life. I knew that, as I have shared with others what He has done in my life, many have been inspired to reach for more. Everywhere I turned, people were living billboards for the campaign, "Gail, write." So, at last, I have.

An interesting event happened after I had written three-fourths of the book. I had laid it down because of a move our family was making. After the move, I stopped writing and questioned my ability to communicate. It was early evening on a Friday night when the phone rang. A friend, who is a leader and public speaker, called. I had not talked to her for some time, and I was pleasantly surprised to hear her voice. "Gail," she said, "Have you finished the book?" I laughed and started in with my reasons and excuses for not finishing. Then she responded, "You are delaying your impact to the nations."

I immediately thought back to something that had challenged my vision only four months previously. A few days before we moved, I was alone for the night in our campus apartment. Most of our furniture had been removed and the rooms were almost empty. My bed was a pallet of blankets on the carpeted floor. Nearby was my clock radio and computer. Tony was away for the night, but he would return in the morning.

I have always been a night owl, and I like to work late hours when everyone is sleeping. However, this particular evening I was exhausted and quickly fell into a deep sleep. Later, I sat up wide-awake, fully rested, and acutely aware that I had been awakened for some specific reason. Someone seemed to stand over me, rousing me out of my slumber. The presence of the Lord, Himself, seemed to be in my room.

Suddenly, I was aware of a song blaring on the radio, and I wondered if I had left it on or if it had been turned on for me. The words not only caught my attention but also pierced my spirit. "Ask me for the nations and I will give them to you as an inheritance and the ends of the earth for your possession." It was as if the Lord had a favorite song that He wanted me to listen to, and so I did.

At the end of the song, I maneuvered through the darkness to my talking computer to find out it was 2:08 in the morning. I had only been asleep for two short hours; yet, I was wide awake and ready to take on the world. I said aloud in the empty room, "Lord, what are you requiring of me?"

I began to pray for eight nations that I have carried in my heart. I asked that revival come within their borders. For the next thirty minutes I worshipped and prayed to the Lord of the Harvest, keenly aware of His love for people. I was in awe that He would share His heart and His song with me. Often, I had quoted the Psalm that declares that God will command His loving kindness in the daytime and give us His song in the night. Unmistakably, I had not only heard His song but also His heart—it was the nations. When I finally lay back down, I returned to a deep sleep.

The following morning when Tony arrived home, I told him about the event in the middle of the night. I had wondered if the time 2:08 a.m. was significant. I asked him if he would read Psalm 2:8 to me. Chills came over me as Tony read, "Ask of Me, and I will give You the nations for Your inheritance, and the ends of the earth for Your possession." Once again I asked, "Lord, what are you requiring of me?"

In an act of obedience, I have taken the time to write this book. It has been painful to revisit stories and emotions that I had suppressed deep in the crevices of my heart. I have found, though, that the heart never forgets. As I have reread chapters, I have been captivated by the thought that the Savior was with me in the midst of each circumstance. My heart's desire is that everyone who reads this chronicle of my life will be encouraged to look beyond today and see heaven's agenda. I contend that everyone has something they are "seeing beyond." Look at the present chapter in your own life, and see beyond its pain, confusion, or even delight, as you find its value. The yesterdays of life have prepared us for today as we reach for tomorrow. All of it is valuable.

What has helped me to see beyond today is my knowing a Savior who has kept His eye on me through every step of the journey. I have come a long way from the little girl who was paid by others to be good in church. Somewhere along the path, I came to see His love and embraced it. I wonder about you? Have you ever seen His eternal love and plan for your life?

Permit me to tell you what I see.

God the Father created mankind in His own image and desired to have fellowship with him. However, man rejected God. The Father, in His mercy, seeing beyond our fatally wrong choice, made provision for us. God sent His only Son, Jesus Christ, to give His life in exchange for ours. At Calvary, Jesus took our sins and forgave them, restoring us to fellowship with our heavenly Father.

When Jesus Christ came to earth, He modeled the heart of the Father as He lived life touching other lives. However, because of the misconceptions of religious leaders and the world, Jesus was brutally murdered on a public cross. He was mocked, and His beard was plucked out. He was beaten with whips, and a crown of thorns was ruthlessly pressed into His skull. He was stripped naked. His hands and feet were nailed to the cross. He was denied water. A filthy sword pierced His side. Even in this condition, Jesus Christ determined to see beyond the agony and violence. In Hebrews, the Bible speaks of Christ, "who for the joy set before Him endured the cross." What on earth could He have seen as He hung there to die for mankind? What was His joy?

You.

You were His joy. Jesus chose to see beyond all the suffering. He saw you in need of a Savior, and He willingly gave His life for you. Seeing beyond the cruelty and darkness of mankind, He chose to see you accepting His love and redemption. Jesus Christ was not only killed and buried, but He also was resurrected after three days. He ascended back to heaven and now is seated at the right hand of His Father.

Now, it is up to you to choose life. Choosing life is your decision. He offers abundant life that is eternal. Simply say, "Yes, Lord Jesus, I receive you as my Savior." The scriptures say, "If you confess with your mouth that Jesus Christ is Lord and believe in your heart that God raised Him from the dead, you will be saved." Simply ask Him to be your Lord.

The grace of the Lord has been my mainstay through all the pages you have just read. I have never really longed for anything my whole life except to serve God and His purposes in my generation. I am passionate about His kingdom and focused on His harvest of souls. My blindness may be evident to those who would study my walk and yet, surprisingly, I see more than many of those around me. The inner vision that God has given me has made all the difference.

I struggled for years over being blind, not wanting to serve my Savior with any handicaps or limitations. I didn't want a barrier between others and me. I did not want to lose my independence. I did not want to be vulnerable. I feared that my infirmity would defame a God who can do the impossible. As I pondered each step along the way, my deepest cry of all was, "Do I have any value?"

In the early years of my progressive loss of eyesight, I could not even say the word "blind," and I did not want others to know that I could not see what they could. Though I had read in the scriptures that in our weakness He is made strong, I did not want to be weak. I had dreams and plans that I wanted to pursue, and blindness was not part of the package. I did not know how to surrender to His complete love. I had underestimated His ability to show me how. In the middle of my struggle, however, I encountered the living Savior who has opened my eyes to see from His perspective.

My prayer is that I walk graciously on this path that is being carved out. I cannot see its end or where the next turn will be, but I am confident that He who walks by my side will direct my steps. I look forward to what comes. In my most vulnerable, broken place, I found grace to embrace the God of Comfort and Hope. May I find His true riches as I see beyond the blindness, anticipating the day I will soon see again. While I wait, I enjoy challenging those with perfect visual acuity to have vision. Anyone can look, but few can "See Beyond."

Seeing Beyond
Scripture References

All Scriptures are from the New King James Version [NKJV].

Preface

Mark 8:18 *"Having eyes, do you not see? And having ears, do you not hear? And do you not remember?"*

Chapter 3

2 Corinthians 12:9 *"And He said to me, 'My grace is sufficient for you, for My strength is made perfect in weakness.' Therefore most gladly I will rather boast in my infirmities, that the power of Christ may rest upon me."*

Chapter 4

Psalm 127:4 *"Like arrows in the hand of a warrior, so are the children of one's youth."*

Chapter 7

Job 13:15a *"Though He slay me, yet will I trust Him."*

Psalm 27:1 *"The LORD is my light and my salvation; whom shall I fear? The LORD is the strength of my life; of whom shall I be afraid?"*

Psalm 23:4 *"Yea, though I walk through the valley of the shadow of death, I will fear no evil; for You are with me; Your rod and Your staff, they comfort me."*

1 Timothy 1:1b *"the Lord Jesus Christ, our hope,"*

Psalm 118:8 *"It is better to trust in the LORD than to put confidence in man."*

2 Corinthians 1:3 *"Blessed be the God and Father of our Lord Jesus Christ, the Father of mercies and God of* all comfort,"

Romans 15:13 *"Now may the God of hope fill you with all joy and peace in believing, that you may abound in hope by the power of the Holy Spirit."*

Hebrews 6:19a *"This* hope *we have as an anchor of the soul, both sure and steadfast,"*

Chapter 8

1 Corinthians 15:55, 57 *"O Death, where is your sting? O Hades, where is your victory?"57 But thanks be to God, who gives us the victory through our Lord Jesus Christ."*

Isaiah 53:4 *"Surely He has borne our griefs and carried our sorrows; yet we esteemed Him stricken, smitten by God, and afflicted."*

Daniel 9:3,23; 10:13 *"Then I set my face toward the Lord God to make request by prayer and supplications, with fasting, sackcloth, and ashes. 23 At the beginning of your supplications the command went out, and I have come to tell you, for you are greatly beloved; therefore consider the matter, and understand the vision: 10:13 But the prince of the kingdom of Persia withstood me twenty-one days; and behold, Michael, one of the chief princes, came to help me, for I had been left alone there with the kings of Persia."*

Chapter 9

Matthew 11:29 *"Take My yoke upon you and learn from me, for I am gentle and lowly in heart, and you will find rest for your souls."*

Chapter 12

Luke 1:38 **"***Then Mary said, "Behold the maidservant of the Lord! Let it be to me according to your word." And the angel departed from her.*

Chapter 13

Psalm 144:12 *"That our sons* may be *as plants grown up in their youth; that our daughters* may be *as pillars, sculptured in palace style;"*

Psalm 78:51 *"And destroyed all the firstborn in Egypt, the first of their strength in the tents of Ham."*

Proverbs 11:3   *"The fruit of the righteous* is a *tree of life, and he who wins souls* is *wise.*

Chapter 14

1 John 4:18 *"There is no fear in love; but perfect love casts out fear, because fear involves torment. But he who fears has not been made perfect in love."*

Psalm 27:1 *"The LORD is my light and my salvation; whom shall I fear? The LORD is the strength of my life; of whom shall I be afraid?"*

Chapter 15

Hebrew 4:1 *"Therefore, since a promise remains of entering His rest, let us fear lest any of you seem to have come short of it."*

John 9:1-3 *"Now as Jesus passed by, He saw a man who was blind from birth. 2 And His disciples asked Him, saying, 'Rabbi, who sinned, this man or his parents, that he was born blind?' 3 Jesus answered, 'Neither this man nor his parents sinned, but that the works of God should be revealed in him.'"*

Psalm 56:8-9 *"You number my wanderings; put my tears into Your bottle; are they not in Your book? 9 When I cry out to you, then my enemies will turn back; this I know, because God is for me."*

Psalm 145:18 *"The LORD is near to all who call upon Him, to all who call upon Him in truth."*

Chapter 17

Psalm 16:5 *"O LORD, You are the portion of my inheritance and my cup; You maintain my lot."*

Chapter 19

Psalm 42:5 *"Why are you cast down, O my soul? And why are you disquieted within me? Hope in God, for I shall yet praise Him for the help of His countenance."*

Psalm 46:1 *"God is our refuge and strength, a very present help in trouble."*

Psalm 119:105 *"Your word is a lamp to my feet and a light to my path."*

Revelation 22:13 *"I am the Alpha and the Omega, the Beginning and the End, the First and the Last."*

Chapter 20

Acts 16:14 *"Now a certain woman named Lydia heard us. She was a seller of purple from the city of Thyatira, who worshiped God. The Lord opened her heart to heed the things spoken by Paul."*

Acts 21:8-9 *"On the next day we who were Paul's companions departed and came to Caesarea, and entered the house of Philip the evangelist, who was one of the seven, and stayed with him. 9 Now this man had four virgin daughters who prophesied."*

Hebrews 11:10 NIV *"For he was looking forward to the city with foundations, whose architect and builder is God."*

Chapter 21

Matthew 10:29-31 *"Are not two sparrows sold for a copper coin? And not one of them falls to the ground apart from your Father's will. 30 But the very hairs of your head are all numbered. 31 Do not fear therefore; you are of more value than many sparrows."*

Genesis 18:12 *"Therefore Sarah laughed within herself, saying, "After I have grown old, shall I have pleasure, my lord being old also?"*

Luke 2:21 *"And when eight days were completed for the circumcision of the Child, His name was called JESUS, the name given by the angel before He was conceived in the womb."*

Chapter 22

Psalm 1:1-2 *"Blessed is the man who walks not in the counsel of the ungodly, nor stands in the path of sinners, nor sits in the seat of the scornful; 2 but his delight is in the law of the LORD, and in His law he meditates day and night."*

Chapter 23

Exodus 22:21 *"You shall neither mistreat a stranger nor oppress him, for you were strangers in the land of Egypt."*

Hebrews 13:2 *"Do not forget to entertain strangers, for by so doing some have unwittingly entertained angels.*

Chapter 25

James 2:17 *"Thus also faith by itself, if it does not have works, is dead."*

Hebrews 11:8-10 *"By faith Abraham obeyed when he was called to go out to the place which he would receive as an inheritance. And he went out, not knowing where he was going. 9 By faith he dwelt in the land of promise as in a foreign country, dwelling in tents with Isaac and Jacob, the heirs with him of the same promise; 10 for he waited for the city which has foundations, whose builder and maker is God."*

Deuteronomy 1:1a, 32:47 *"These are the words Moses spoke to all Israel in the desert east of the Jordan...32:47 'They are not just idle words—they are your life. By them you will live long in the land you are crossing the Jordan to possess.'"*

Matthew 5:13-*14 "You are the salt of the earth; but if the salt loses its flavor, how shall it be seasoned? It is then good for nothing but to be thrown out and trampled underfoot by men. 14 "You are the light of the world. A city that is set on a hill cannot be hidden."*

Chapter 26

Psalm 23:4 *"Yea, though I walk through the valley of the shadow of death, I will fear no evil; for You are with me; Your rod and Your staff, they comfort me."*

Psalm 31:14-15 *"But as for me, I trust in You, O LORD; I say, 'You are my God.' 15 My times are in Your hand; Deliver me from the hand of my enemies, and from those who persecute me."*

Chapter 27

Luke 23:34 *"Then Jesus said, 'Father, forgive them, for they do not know what they do.' And they divided His garments and cast lots."*

Chapter 28

2 Corinthians 12:9 *"And He said to me, 'My grace is sufficient for you, for My strength is made perfect in weakness.' Therefore most gladly I will rather boast in my infirmities, that the power of Christ may rest upon me."*

Chapter 29

1 Corinthians 10:13 *"No temptation has overtaken you except such as is common to man; but God is faithful, who will not allow you to be tempted beyond what you are able, but with the temptation will also make the way of escape, that you may be able to bear it."*

2 Timothy 1:12 *"For this reason I also suffer these things; nevertheless I am not ashamed, for I know whom I have believed and am persuaded that He is able to keep what I have committed to Him until that Day."*

Chapter 30

Deuteronomy 30:19 *"I call heaven and earth as witnesses today against you, that I have set before you life and death, blessing and cursing; therefore choose life, that both you and your descendants may live;"*

Deuteronomy 31:8 *"And the LORD, He is the One who goes before you. He will be with you, He will not leave you nor forsake you; do not fear nor be dismayed."*

John 3:16 *"For God so loved the world that He gave His only begotten Son, that whoever believes in Him should not perish but have everlasting life."*

1 John 3:1 *"Behold what manner of love the Father has bestowed on us, that we should be called children of God! Therefore the world does not know us, because it did not know Him."*

Genesis 1:27 *"So God created man in His own image; in the image of God He created him; male and female He created them."*

Colossians 1:21-22 *"And you, who once were alienated and enemies in your mind by wicked works, yet now He has reconciled 22 in the body of His flesh through death, to present you holy, and blameless, and above reproach in His sight."*

John 14:9-10 *"Jesus said to him, 'Have I been with you so long, and yet you have not known Me, Philip? He who has seen Me has seen the Father; so how can you say, 'Show us the Father'? 10 Do you not believe that I am in the Father, and the Father in Me? The words that I speak to you I do not speak on My own authority; but the Father who dwells in Me does the works.'"*

Isaiah 50:6 *"I gave My back to those who struck Me, and My cheeks to those who plucked out the beard; I did not hide My face from shame and spitting."* (Ref: John 19:1-20:18; Psalm 22:6,7,16,18)

Isaiah 53:5 *"But He was wounded for our transgressions, He was bruised for our iniquities; the chastisement for our peace was upon Him, and by His stripes we are healed."*

Hebrews 12:2 *"Looking unto Jesus, the author and finisher of our faith, who for the joy that was set before Him endured the cross, despising the shame, and has sat down at the right hand of the throne of God."*

John 15:10-11 *"If you keep My commandments, you will abide in My love, just as I have kept My Father's commandments and abide in His love. 11 "These things I have spoken to you, that My joy may remain in you, and that your joy may be full."*

Acts 1:9-10 *"Now when He had spoken these things, while they watched, He was taken up, and a cloud received Him out of their sight. 10 And while they looked steadfastly toward heaven as He went up, behold, two men stood by them in white apparel,"*

Romans 8:34 *"...It is Christ who died, and furthermore is also risen, who is even at the right hand of God, who also makes intercession for us."*

Deuteronomy 30:19 *"I call heaven and earth as witnesses today against you, that I have set before you life and death, blessing and cursing; therefore choose life, that both you and your descendants may live;"*

John 3:16 *"For God so loved the world that He gave His only begotten Son, that whoever believes in Him should not perish but have everlasting life."*
Romans 10:9 *"that if you confess with your mouth the Lord Jesus and believe in your heart that God has raised Him from the dead, you will be saved."*

Acts 13:36 NIV *"For when David had served God's purpose in his own generation, he fell asleep; he was buried with his fathers..."*

Luke 1:37 *"For with God nothing will be impossible."*

2 Corinthians 12:9 *"And He said to me, 'My grace is sufficient for you, for My strength is made perfect in weakness.' Therefore most gladly I will rather boast in my infirmities, that the power of Christ may rest upon me."*

John 14:23 *"Jesus answered and said to him, 'If anyone loves Me, he will keep My word; and My Father will love him, and We will come to him and make Our home with him.'"*

Psalm 37:23-24 *"The steps of a good man are ordered by the LORD, and He delights in his way. 24 Though he fall, he shall not be utterly cast down; for the LORD upholds him with His hand."*

Hebrews 4:16 *"Let us therefore come boldly to the throne of grace, that we may obtain mercy and find grace to help in time of need."*

2 Corinthians 1:3 *"Blessed be the God and Father of our Lord Jesus Christ, the Father of mercies and God of all comfort,"*

Romans 15:13 *"Now may the God of hope fill you with all joy and peace in believing, that you may abound in hope by the power of the Holy Spirit."*

Proverbs 22:4 *"By humility and the fear of the LORD are riches and honor and life."*

2 Corinthians 4:18 *"while we do not look at the things which are seen, but at the things which are not seen. For the things which are seen are temporary, but the things which are not seen are eternal."*

ABOUT THE AUTHOR

Gail McWilliams is a vivacious and humorous speaker, author, and national radio host. She will inspire and encourage you to run the race that is set before you with joy. Her experience also includes being a pastor's wife and a television co-host. She couples real life with Biblical principles that help you see more clearly. Her personal story of how she lost her eyesight will amaze you and also challenge you to develop a bigger vision and purpose for life. Her optimistic and realistic approach encourages others to believe that God will provide strength and peace in difficult circumstances. She expresses an overcoming spirit along with a down-to-earth sincerity. Her life conveys that having vision makes all the difference.

She lives in Texas with her husband, Tony, and their children and grandchildren.

CONTACT THE AUTHOR
Gail McWilliams can be contacted for bookings at
www.GailMcWilliams.com